Roman Catholicism

Roman Catholicism

A Contemporary Evangelical Perspective

Paul G. Schrotenboer

BAKER BOOK HOUSE
Grand Rapids, Michigan 49516

Reprinted 1988 by
Baker Book House with permission

Chapters 1–9 and the conclusion first appeared in *The Evangelical Review of Theology* 10, 4 (1986); 11, 1, (1987).

Library of Congress Cataloging-in-Publication Data

Roman Catholicism.

    Reprint. Originally published: Singapore: World Evangelical Fellowship, ©1987.
    Bibliography: p.
    Includes index.
    1. Catholic Church—Doctrines. 2. Evangelicalism—Relations—Catholic Church. 3. Catholic Church—Relations—Evangelicalism. I. Schrotenboer, Paul G.
BX1751.2.R65   1988   282   88-24175
ISBN 0-8010-8292-7

Contents

79729

Preface

The Roman Catholic Church, long considered impervious to change, has in recent time undergone widespread changes. Some of these are official, others are local, but all of them are significant. The Roman Catholic Church is neither the monolith it was once thought to be nor an immovable object.

As the pages of this book show, changes in Roman Catholicism include the Catholic opinion of non-Roman churches and of non-Christian religions, as well as her views on religious liberty and the promotion of social justice.

Besides the many facets of change in Roman Catholic position and policy, many different faces of Rome are manifested in different parts of the world. Catholicism that manifests a crucified Christ and a robust Virgin in Mexico is a far cry from Catholicism in the Netherlands with its high view of faith and lesser emphasis on Mary. The Bible movement, the charismatic groups, the base communities, the widespread use of contraceptives among Catholics in North America, all testify to the variety of ways in which the Church of Rome presents itself today.

At the same time there are many indications that Rome is fundamentally the same as it has always been. Paul VI clearly stated in 1964 that "nothing really changes in the traditional doctrine." John

Paul II has on many fronts vigorously stressed a stronger sense of self-identity among Catholics, particularly in personal ethics and in Mariology. In October 1986 in Assisi he called for a world day of prayer for peace, inviting representatives not only from other Christian communions but also from other religions. In early 1987 he proclaimed the Marian year and issued his encyclical *Redemptoris Mater.*

When evangelical Christians view this changing scene and note the continuity from one century and one pope to another, as well as the variety of manifestations of the church, they understandably assess the Roman Catholic Church differently. Those whose families have been oppressed by Catholic priests find it difficult, in spite of the declaration on religious liberty, to acknowledge basic changes for the better. Those who cooperate for social justice with leaders in the base communities take a more positive view. On the personal level Protestants and Roman Catholics can share fellowship in faith in Jesus Christ as Savior and Lord. On the social level many evangelicals find an ally in the Church of Rome in the efforts to promote equity in education and the protection of the unborn. On the local level much depends on whether the Roman Church is a dominant social force or an uninfluential minority; or whether, as one of many churches in a nation, it shares the general ethos of civil liberty.

This document by evangelicals about Roman Catholicism is designed to clarify the relationship of evangelical Christians to Roman Catholic faith and practice. The occasion for drafting it was a potentially divisive difference of opinion among evangelicals at the General Assembly of the World Evangelical Fellowship (WEF) in Hoddesdon, England, in 1980.

General Secretary Waldron Scott, with clearance from the executive council, had invited two observers from the Roman Catholic Church to attend the assembly. Mr. Ralph Martin, a leader in the Roman Catholic charismatic renewal movement, and Msgr. Basil Meeking of the Vatican Secretariat for Promoting Christian Unity were present and brought greetings from the platform.

This led to heated discussion, an apology by General Secretary Scott, and action to require representatives or observers from ecclesiastical, ecumenical, or political bodies to future general assemblies to be approved in advance by a majority of the full WEF membership. In spite of this, the Italian Evangelical Alliance withdrew its membership, and the Spanish Evangelical Alliance placed its participation in abeyance.

The WEF Theological Commission responded by creating a seventeen-member Ecumenical Issues Task Force and assigning it to forge a statement of evangelical stance toward Roman Catholicism that all member bodies of the fellowship could endorse. With three members each appointed from Italy and Spain, the task force was weighted to give adequate attention to their grievances.

The task force spent two years preparing, circulating, and critiquing a series of three study drafts. It then spent a week in Madrid in October 1985 working through the third draft sentence by sentence and making numerous adjustments in detail. This revised draft was then circulated to all the members of the study group.

Delegates to the fellowship's Eighth General Assembly in Singapore in June 1986 discussed and overwhelmingly approved the document as presented by the task force. Out of some eighty-nine delegates, there was one negative vote and one abstention. The action was to adopt the document reproduced on the following pages and to recommend it to the constituent members of the World Evangelical Fellowship.

The task force that wrote the document was asked to prepare a position statement with which evangelicals could identify and that would heal the breach that had occurred. For this reason the document was designed specifically for consolidation and healing among evangelicals concerning the Church of Rome.

People who were not aware of the dynamics within the WEF have questioned why direct dialogue was not sought with spokespersons of the Vatican. Some have judged that the lack of discussion with Rome at this point was a regrettable omission. I do not share that opinion.

My reason is existential in nature; in some areas, such as in Italy, Spain, and parts of Latin America, evangelicals who were formerly nominal Roman Catholics feel painfully and personally that they have been mistreated by Roman Catholic officials. They are concerned that if they had not broken with the church with its stress on human merit and the priesthood as the purveyor of grace, they would never have come to a saving faith in Jesus Christ. For such persons the time was simply not opportune to discuss theology with representatives of Rome. Before fruitful dialogue could take place, certain preconditions had to be met.

The first of these was an evangelical consensus about Roman Catholicism. Along with such a consensus could come a heightened sense of evangelical self-identity. As such, then, they could eventually in a sense meet as equals. They could speak from a position of clarity, even as Rome could clearly state what its teachings are. But for a party to dialogue with another before it reaches clarity on what it believes is to invite disaster.

A second requirement, flowing from the first, was the strengthening of mutual trust among evangelicals. This, I am pleased to report, has very largely been achieved.

This does not mean that dialogue between evangelicals and Roman Catholics should continue to be discouraged. On the contrary, the remarkable consensus that was manifested in Singapore in 1986 provides a basis on which dialogue can and should be undertaken. For it was there that agreement was reached and trust was restored.

Dialogue could well be the next step. Actually, one of the representatives of the Italian Evangelical Alliance at the WEF General Assembly in Singapore who had had deep misgivings about the events in Hoddesdon stated that with this document in hand evangelicals in Italy could with confidence engage in discussion with representatives of Rome.

This is the challenge to evangelicals arising from the present changing situation. There is much to give us hope for reformation according to the Word of God in the Church of Rome. There is also much in the recent reaffirmations of Roman Catholicism to give us pause in believing that all basic differences will soon have been removed.

The challenge is to bear witness to the faith once for all entrusted to the people of God (Jude 3) and to be honest and open in recognizing both agreements and departures from this faith. In that challenge *Roman Catholicism: A Contemporary Evangelical Perspective* can play an important role.

Paul G. Schrotenboer

Contributors

Henri Blocher teaches theology at the Theological College of Vaux-sur-Seine, France.

Pietro Bolognesi is director of the Istituto Evangelico, Rome, Italy.

Samuel Escobar teaches theology at the Eastern Baptist Theological Seminary, Lancaster, Pennsylvania.

Juan Gili is director of Evangelismo en Accion, Madrid, Spain.

Jose M. Martinez is theological secretary of the Spanish Evangelical Alliance, Barcelona, Spain.

Elio Milazzo is president of the Italian Evangelical Alliance, Florence, Italy.

Emilio Antonio Nunez is professor at Seminario Theologico Centroamerico, Guatemala City, Guatemala.

Pablo Perez is executive secretary of the World Evangelical Fellowship Commission on Church Renewal, Dallas, Texas.

Paul G. Schrotenboer is general secretary of the Reformed Ecumenical Synod, Grand Rapids, Michigan.

Gordon Spykman is professor of theology and religion at Calvin College, Grand Rapids, Michigan.

Sunand Sumithra is executive secretary of the Theological Commission of the World Evangelical Fellowship, Bangalore, India.

Terry (Pablo) Wickham is missionary of the Spanish Evangelical Church, Madrid, Spain.

Introduction

We as the World Evangelical Fellowship confess wholeheartedly our commitment to the evangelical faith. We stand together upon the Word of God embodied in the witness of the prophets and the apostles. We draw our strength from the gospel of Jesus Christ, our Savior and Lord. We acknowledge our deep indebtedness to the historic Christian faith rearticulated in the heritage of the sixteenth-century Reformation. This is the common ground that sustains our fellowship. These are our credentials. Therein lies our identity and our reason for existence. Thus united, we seek the promised leading of the Holy Spirit in nurturing our fellowship and defining our common mission in the world. In common faith and mutual trust we seek to fulfil our God-given calling to proclaim the gospel and to serve as agents of reconciliation in a broken world.

Standing within this rich tradition, we now face the enormous spiritual challenges of our day. Looming large among them is the ongoing urgent task to clarify our relationship to Roman Catholic faith and practice. During the past centuries, and especially in recent decades, significant changes are evident along many fronts. There is great ferment in Roman Catholic circles and the picture is far from clear. In it all we welcome every hopeful sign pointing to the revival of true apostolic faith. We experience continuing dismay, however, whenever the gospel is blurred or eclipsed. It seems sometimes that everything is changing, when at times nothing has changed. Clearly the central issues of the sixteenth-century struggles are still very much alive among the heirs of both Rome and the Reformation.

In the midst of these contemporary vortices we reaffirm the fundamental truths of the way of salvation as formulated by the Reformers. Our rule for faith and life is *sola Scriptura*. The work of atonement was wrought *solo Christo*. We are adopted as children of God *sola gratia*. Our justification is *sola fide*. Our worship and service is *soli Deo gloria*.

In working out the implications of these common convictions, we must learn together to practice the truth in the spirit of love. Our fellowship embraces Christians from many different ethnic, national, and cultural situations. Our far-flung churches are called to live out the Christian faith under sharply contrasting circumstances. We must therefore demonstrate mutual trust as together we rely on God's presence and power to keep us all faithfully and fruitfully active in the various sectors of his kingdom. We must exercise understanding and restraint lest our fellowship impose upon brothers and sisters elsewhere burdens that neither they nor we are able to bear under the given circumstances.

In the spirit of Christian discipleship we must be careful not to allow internal strife and dissension to obstruct the ministry to which God calls us in his world. We must keep the avenues of service open to the work of the Holy Spirit so that he can accomplish his purposes in the lives of people and in the institutions of society that are sensitive to his Word. For we live in a world where millions are strangers to the gospel and other millions, nominally Christians, are in need of evangelizing. We may not compromise the essentials of the gospel; we cannot afford to harbor tensions and divisions that stand as obstacles in the path of our mission.

Our solidarity in the confession of our faith as expressed in the WEF Statement of Faith shapes our approach to Roman Catholicism.[1] Standing strong in Christ, we can share the treasures of the gospel in candid and fearless contact with the Church of Rome. Such actions must be motivated by commitment to the truth. And mutual love constrains us to reach out

1. We believe in (1) *the Holy Scriptures* as originally given by God, divinely inspired, infallible, entirely trustworthy, and the supreme authority in all matters of faith and conduct; (2) *one God*, eternally existent in three persons, Father, Son, and Holy Spirit; (3) *our Lord Jesus Christ*, God manifest in the flesh, his virgin birth, his sinless human life, his divine miracles, his vicarious and atoning death, his bodily resurrection, his ascension, his mediatorial work, and his personal return in power and glory; (4) *the salvation* of lost and sinful man through the shed blood of the Lord Jesus Christ by faith apart from works, and regeneration by the Holy Spirit; (5) *the Holy Spirit* by whose indwelling the believer is enabled to live a holy life, to witness and work for the Lord Jesus Christ; (6) *the unity of the Spirit* of all true believers, the church, the body of Christ; (7) *the resurrection* of both the saved and the lost; they that are saved unto the resurrection of life, they that are lost unto the resurrection of damnation.

to others. This challenge is inescapable, given the large role that the Roman Catholic Church plays as a very formative social and political reality in many nations. Our actions must indeed be guided by faithfulness to the gospel. But such faithfulness should reckon with the great diversities that manifest themselves currently in Roman Catholic popular piety, style of worship, church rule, and understanding of doctrine—even though the binding authority of the dogmatic declarations issued by her central teaching authority ultimately lay their claim upon all her followers. All diversities, both within the Roman Catholic Church and the World Evangelical Fellowship, must be judged by the light of the Scriptures.

In our consideration of Roman Catholicism, some aspects of the contemporary spiritual condition of the world demand special attention from evangelical leaders and pastors all over the world.

1. The growth and spread of secularism and anti-Christian ideologies in an increasingly hostile world have produced among some Christians an increased sense of urgency concerning the need for cooperation and unity between different churches.

2. The wide and intelligent use of mass media by the Roman Catholic Church, as well as the particular gifts that the present pope has for public exposure, has projected to the world a completely new image of the Roman Catholic Church as an institution that is very attractive.

3. In Protestantism there has been a formidable growth of independent churches, new evangelical denominations, and parachurch movements. Many of these bodies are not clearly conscious of the doctrinal heritage of the Reformation and consequently of the sharp doctrinal differences between Roman Catholics and evangelicals. This goes along with the ahistorical and antirational stance of vast segments of the population in contemporary society.

4. The clear anti-Marxist stance of the present pope has provided Catholicism with a new ground for acceptance even among Protestant or evangelical persons in North America and Europe. This acceptance on ideological grounds often does not take into account the demands of evangelical truth.

All these factors produce confusion, ambiguous schemes of cooperation, deceptive experiences and an abandonment of evangelical truth. These factors also constitute the rationale for this statement. They require that as evangelicals we not only consider our relation to the Church of Rome, but also that we clarify the doctrinal issues for ourselves and act in harmony with our confession.

Obviously, our study cannot cover all aspects of church doctrine and life. We have therefore decided to limit this initial statement to nine areas of particular importance to evangelical Christians, especially in countries where they are a minority among Catholics.

1. Other Churches
2. Religious Liberty
3. The Place of Mary
4. Authority in the Church
5. The Pope and Infallibility
6. Modernism and Theological Liberalism
7. Justification by Faith Alone
8. Sacramentalism and the Eucharist
9. The Mission of the Church

1

Other Churches

According to Catholic teaching,[1] the church is Jesus Christ "available" to the point that the church exists alongside of Christ, almost like a second person of Christ ("quasi altera Christi persona," *Mistici Corporis*). As such it is necessary to salvation (*Lumen Gentium*, 14). This idea is very old and widespread in Roman Catholicism. When Paul VI promulgated the constitution *De Ecclesia*, he affirmed that "nothing really changes in the traditional doctrine" (*Osservatore Romano*, no. 22, 1964).

In its Dogmatic Constitution on the Church, Vatican II speaks first of the mystery of the church (chap. 1) and the church as the people of God (chap. 2). It then proceeds to the hierarchy of the church (chap. 3), in which the power and infallibility

1. Vatican II distinguished clearly between the Church of Rome's relation to the Orthodox churches and the churches of the Reformation. Her relation to the Orthodox churches is formulated in the Decree on Eastern Catholic Churches. Our remarks are limited to the relation of the Church of Rome to Protestant churches and are based largely on the Decree on the Church (*Lumen Gentium*) and the Decree on Ecumenism (*De Ecumenismo*).

of the pope are set forth and the basis is laid for the church's relation to other churches. Our assessment of the role of the Church of Rome in the ecumenical movement should be based, however, not only on the church's official teaching, but also on the way it presents itself in different areas of the world. The relation of the Church of Rome to the churches of the Reformation has been a real concern to evangelical Christians for many years, even centuries. This is especially true in nations where Catholicism has been the dominant religion. In most of these nations the Church of Rome has held a privileged position with the civil government, and the evangelical churches have often been oppressed and marginalized in the exercise of their religion and in their civil rights.

In recent decades some significant changes have taken place, both in practice and in teaching, in Rome's relation to other churches.

Yet the assumption throughout the documents of Vatican II is that the Church of Rome is the one true church. This appears from the statement that the one holy catholic and apostolic church "subsists in the Catholic Church, which is governed by the successor of Peter and by the bishops in union with this successor . . ." (*Lumen Gentium*, 8). This church, the body of the faithful as a whole, anointed as they are by the Holy Spirit (cf. 1 John 2:20, 27), cannot err in matters of belief (*Lumen Gentium*, 12). The church clings without fail to the faith under the lead of a sacred teaching authority to which it loyally defers (*Lumen Gentium*, 12). This assumption may also be seen to underlie the statement that whoever refuses to enter or remain in the Catholic church cannot be saved (*Lumen Gentium*, 14).

That Rome considers itself the one true church does not mean that it claims that the other churches (ecclesial communities) are devoid of all the marks of the church. Nor does it speak of these ecclesial communions in a haughty manner. Vatican II made it clear that the separated churches bear many of the qualities of the church. It recognized that all who are justified by faith through baptism are brothers in the Lord (*De Ecumenismo*, 3), that all endowments that build up the church can exist outside the visible boundaries of the Catholic church (*De Ecumenismo*, 3), that "brethren divided from us" also carry out many of the sacred actions of the Christian religion (*De Ecumenismo*, 3), and that the Holy Spirit is at work in these ecclesial communities.

In a key paragraph Vatican II said that "[the] separated Churches and Communities, though we believe they suffer from defects already mentioned, have by no means been deprived of significance and importance in the mystery of salvation. For the Spirit of Christ has not refrained from using them as means of salvation which derive their efficacy from the very fullness of grace and truth entrusted to the Catholic Church" (*De Ecumenismo*, 3).

Yet, given these qualifications, there is an essential difference between the Church of Rome and the other churches.

> . . . [O]ur separated brethren, whether considered as individuals or as Communities and Churches, are

not blessed with that unity which Jesus Christ
wished to bestow on all those whom He has regen-
erated and vivified into one body and newness of
life—that unity which the holy Scriptures and the
revered tradition of the Church proclaim. For it is
through Christ's Catholic Church alone, which is the
all-embracing means of salvation, that the fullness
of the means of salvation can be obtained. It was to
the apostolic college alone, of which Peter is the
head, that we believe our Lord entrusted all the
blessings of the New Covenant, in order to establish
on earth the one Body of Christ into which all those
should be fully incorporated who already belong in
any way to God's People (*De Ecumenismo*, 3).

The Church of Rome is ready to grant that people
on both sides were to blame for the divisions in the
church and that the church always has need of con-
tinual reformation, but she insists that the way to
true unity of the world leads to Rome. "As the obstacles to perfect ecclesiastical communion are overcome, all Christians will be gathered, in a common
celebration of the Eucharist, into that unity of the
one and only Church which Christ bestowed on His
Church from the beginning. This unity, we believe,
subsists in the [Roman] Catholic Church as some-
thing she can never lose, and we hope that it will
continue to increase until the end of time" (*De
Ecumenismo*, 4).

Moreover, all the endowments possessed by those
outside the Catholic church "by right belong to the
one Church of Christ." It is into the Church of Rome
then that all those people who belong in any way to

God's people should be incorporated (*De Ecumenismo*, 3).

It is widely held that an ecumenical council of the churches will be needed to restore unity to the world church. But Rome makes clear that it is the "prerogative of the Roman Pontiff to convoke these Councils, to preside over them, and to confirm them" (*Lumen Gentium*, 22). The call to Rome is no longer in imperial tones, but it is unmistakably present.

Evangelicals have reason to be glad that the former hard line of the Church of Rome regarding the churches of the Reformation has been modified as indicated by Vatican II. They also appreciate the willingness of the Church of Rome to enter into discussion with theologians of various confessions on an equal basis. Evangelicals, however, are not prepared to accept the claim that the Church of Rome is the one only true church, nor that its supreme teaching office is free from all error in matters of belief, nor that the road that leads to Rome is the way to unity.

In the early sixties there was a widespread optimism (although not without deep misgivings from many quarters, especially among evangelicals in Latin America and Latin Europe) concerning the new approach of John XXIII to open the windows of the Church of Rome to the world, to alter the church's view of the "separated," and to engage more vigorously in the activities of the ecumenical movement. But many of these expectations remain largely unfulfilled.

The present stance of the Roman Catholic Church is perhaps best expressed in the address of Pope John

Paul II at the Ecumenical Centre in Geneva on
June 12, 1984:

> When the Catholic Church enters on the difficult
> task of ecumenism, it brings with it a firm convic-
> tion. Despite the moral afflictions which have
> marked the life of its members and even of its lead-
> ers in the course of history, it is convinced that in
> the ministry of the bishop of Rome it has preserved
> the visible focus and guarantee of unity in full fi-
> delity to the apostolic tradition and to the faith of
> the Fathers. St. Ignatius of Antioch in his time
> greeted the Church "which presides in the region of
> the Romans" as that "which presides in charity"
> over the communion. The Catholic Church believes
> that the bishop who presides over the life of that
> local Church made fruitful by the blood of Peter and
> Paul, receives from the Lord the mission to be the
> enduring witness to the faith confessed by these two
> leaders of the apostolic community which, by the
> grace of the Holy Spirit, constitutes the unity of be-
> lievers. To be in communion with the Bishop of Rome
> is to bear visible witness that one is in communion
> with all who confess that same faith, with those who
> have confessed it since Pentecost, and with those
> who will confess it until the Day of the Lord shall
> come. That is our conviction as Catholics and our
> faithfulness to Christ forbids us to relinquish it. We
> also know that this constitutes a difficulty for most
> of you, whose memories are perhaps marked by cer-
> tain painful recollections for which my predecessor
> Pope Paul VI asked your forgiveness. But we have to
> discuss this in all frankness and friendship . . . (World
> Council of Churches Central Committee, Document
> no. 4.9.2, 9–18, July 1984).

From the actions of Pope John Paul II many infer that the Church of Rome is backing off somewhat from its new openness to the other churches, has re-affirmed certain teachings that evangelicals find without biblical warrant, and has come to reassert the fundamental sense of Roman Catholic self-identity. Relations with the World Council of Churches have cooled somewhat. If the only choice for Protestants is either to return to Rome or to continue their separate existence, for the time being many feel compelled to do the latter, even while they hope for greater openness on the part of the Church of Rome and while they on their part strive more earnestly to heal the divisions which they believe they must overcome.

We as evangelicals believe that we should work more earnestly to manifest visibly the oneness of the church of Jesus Christ and are convinced that our unity is a unity in truth. As we consider the teaching and practice of the Church of Rome concerning other churches we are faced with a fundamental question: Should we enter into any relationship at all with the Church of Rome? And, given an affirmative answer, What kind of relationship should this be? This is a crucial and potentially divisive issue. At stake here is the essential confession of what the church is, and also the question present here is, Can we recognize the Church of Rome as a church in the biblical sense?

2

Religious Liberty

One grievance of long standing that evangelicals have against the Church of Rome is that this church, which assumes that it is the one true church, has often not recognized the right of other Christian churches to enjoy full religious freedom. This grievance deserves to be heard. The question is, Has Vatican II made significant changes in the church's teaching on religious liberty? And has the practice of the church changed greatly since pre–Vatican II days? It is necessary to look briefly at this issue.

Religious freedom, according to Vatican II,

> means that all men are to be immune from coercion on the part of individuals or of social groups and of any human power, in such wise that in matters religious no one is to be forced to act in a manner contrary to his own beliefs. Nor is anyone to be restrained from acting in accordance with his own beliefs, whether privately or publicly, whether alone or in association with others, within due limits.
>
> The Synod further declares that the right to religious freedom has its foundation in the very dignity of the human person, as this dignity is known through the revealed Word of God and by reason

itself. This right of the human person to religious freedom is to be recognized in the constitutional law whereby society is governed. Thus it is to become a civil right (*Declaration on Religious Freedom*, 2).

This statement does not mean, however, that all churches and their members should be accorded exactly the same freedom. For, as a footnote to this declaration states,

The Catholic Church claims freedom from coercive interference in her ministry and life on grounds of the divine mandate laid upon her by Christ Himself. . . . It is Catholic faith that no other Church or Community may claim to possess this mandate in all its fulness. In this sense, the freedom of the Church is unique, proper to herself alone, by reason of its foundation. In the case of other religious Communities, the foundation of the right is the dignity of the human person, which requires that men be kept free from coercion, when they act in community, gathered into Churches, as well as when they act alone (*Documents of Vatican II*, p. 682).

Vatican II further acknowledged that the government should

create conditions favorable to the fostering of religious life, in order that the people may be truly enabled to exercise their religious rights and to fulfill their religious duties. . . .

If, in view of peculiar circumstances obtaining among certain peoples, special legal recognition is given in the constitutional order of society to one religious body, it is at the same time imperative that the right of all citizens and religious bodies to reli-

gious freedom should be recognized and made ef-
fective in practice (*Documents of Vatican II*, p. 685).

One might conclude from these declarations that
the Church of Rome, if it is true to this statement,
will not deal with the religious rights of people in
terms of a double standard, demanding freedom when
Roman Catholics are a minority or when they suffer
discrimination by the states, and exacting privilege
for itself and intolerance for others when Roman
Catholics are a majority. The question remains, however, whether the practice of the Church of Rome
agrees with the principle thus expressed.

3

The Place of Mary

There is no question that the place of Mary in
Roman Catholicism is unique. Large areas of both
Roman doctrine and practice are related to her in
many ways. The views on Mary range from the
strictly theological through the highly mystical and
devotional to the rather ordinary and mundane. She
has been exalted above every saint, institution, apostle, or doctrinal expression to the point where, although officially she "neither takes away anything
from nor adds anything to the dignity and efficacy of
Christ the one Mediator," yet in effect many Roman
Catholics put her on the same level as the persons of
the Trinity. All of these perceptions of Mary make
Mariology a major point of controversy between Roman Catholics and evangelicals.

The role of Mary in Roman Catholic teaching and
practice is related to this church's understanding of
itself, to which we have referred in chapter 1. Here
it is important to note that the Church of Rome views
itself as "one interlocked reality which is comprised
of a divine and a human element" (*De Ecclesia*, 8),
in which the mystery of the synthesis of the human
and the divine is realized. The church itself in the

31

teaching of Rome is a sacramental reality, in that it is regarded as the historical extension of the incarnation.

In this perspective it is also possible to understand the importance of Mary for the theology of Rome. For, since Mary is a picture of the church, in exalting Mary, the Roman Catholic Church also exalts itself.

The place of Mary is related further to that of the saints in general. Like the saints, she is to be venerated, only in greater measure. At the Second Council of Nicea (787) a distinction was made between the veneration due to the saints (*dulia*) and the worship (*latria*) due to God alone. Already then Mary was regarded as being in a class by herself, and the veneration given to her was called *huperdulia*. She was thereby placed above the other saints, but below God. The careful distinctions made by theologians, however, are usually not reflected in the practice of the faithful. Gradually Mary came to be regarded not only as a witness to the gospel, an example to follow, but also as a "supernatural friend" who could help in the difficulties of life.

The development of the unique place and role of Mary in Roman Catholicism has its long and deep roots in the history of especially Eastern but also Western Christianity. Marian folklore, rituals, and festivals thrived in many circles as the early church spread over the Mediterranean world and into Europe. Along the way popular practices usually paved the way for official statements of dogma. The phrase *theotokos*, traceable to the councils of Ephesus (431) and Chalcedon (451), was originally used in the context of Christology to affirm the true humanity of our Lord. In time it underwent a radical shift, however, serving eventually to elevate Mary as "Mother of God." By the medieval era the piety, art, and architecture of the "mother church" was saturated with devotion to the Madonna. By the sixteenth century, as evidenced by the spiritual struggles of the Reformers, the image of Mary had largely eclipsed the centrality of Jesus Christ in the life of believers. This distortion was one significant impulse behind the Reformation movement. In its Counter-Reformational response, the Council of Trent (1546–63) declared Mary's sinlessness and perpetual virginity. A further decisive step in the development of Marian dogma was taken in 1854 with the promulgation of the papal bull, *Ineffabilis Deus*. In it Pius IX declared the immaculate conception of the ever-blessed Virgin Mary. This dogma is now binding on all Roman Catholic faithful. Its core passage reads as follows:

> To the glory of the holy and undivided Trinity, to the honour and renown of the Virgin Mother of God, the exaltation of the Catholic faith and the increase of the Christian religion; by the authority of our Lord Jesus Christ, of the blessed apostles Peter and Paul, and by our own authority, we declare, pronounce and define: the doctrine which holds that the most Blessed Virgin Mary was, from the first moment in her conception, by the singular grace and privilege of almighty God and view of the merits of Christ Jesus the Saviour of the human race, preserved immune from all stain of original sin, is revealed by God and, therefore, firmly and con-

stantly to be believed by all the faithful. If, therefore,
any persons shall dare to think otherwise—which
may God forbid—than has been defined by us, let
them clearly know that they stand condemned by
their own judgment, that they have made shipwreck
of their faith and fallen from the unity of the Church.
Furthermore, they subject themselves *ipso facto* to
the penalties provided by law if by speech or writing
or in any other exterior way they shall dare to express their views.

This dogma was then endorsed by Vatican I in 1870.

Another major development in the Marian dogma
came nearly a century later when on November 1,
1950, Pope Pius XII defined in *Munificentissimus Deus*
the dogma of the heavenly assumption of the Blessed
Virgin Mary. Here the key passage reads:

From all eternity and by one and the same decree
of predestination the august Mother of God is united
in a sublime way with Jesus Christ; immaculate in
her conception, a spotless virgin in her divine motherhood, the noble companion of the divine Redeemer who won a complete triumph over sin and
its consequences, she finally obtained as the crown-
ing glory of her privileges to be preserved from the
corruption of the tomb and, like her Son before her,
to conquer death and to be raised body and soul to
the glory of heaven, to shine refulgent as Queen at
the right hand of her Son, the immortal King of ages
(cf. 1 Tim. 1:17).

The universal Church, in which the Spirit of truth
actively dwells, and which is infallibly guided by
Him to an ever more perfect knowledge of revealed

truths, has down the centuries manifested her belief in many ways; the bishops from all over the world ask almost unanimously that the truth of the bodily Assumption of the Blessed Virgin Mary into heaven be defined as a dogma of divine and catholic faith; this truth is based on Sacred Scripture and deeply embedded in the minds of the faithful; it has received the approval of liturgical worship from the earliest times; it is perfectly in keeping with the rest of revealed truth, and has been lucidly developed and explained by the studies, the knowledge and wisdom of theologians. Considering all these reasons we deem that the moment pre-ordained in the plan of divine providence has now arrived for us to proclaim solemnly this extraordinary privilege of the Virgin Mary. . . .

Therefore, having directed humble and repeated prayers to God, and having invoked the light of the Spirit of truth; to the glory of almighty God who has bestowed His special bounty on the Virgin Mary, for the honour of His Son the immortal King of ages and victor over sin and death, for the greater glory of His august mother, and for the joy and exultation of the whole Church; by the authority of our Lord Jesus Christ, of the blessed apostles Peter and Paul, and by our own authority, we proclaim, declare and define as a dogma revealed by God: the Immaculate Mother of God, Mary ever Virgin, when the course of her earthly life was finished, was taken up body and soul into the glory of heaven.

Wherefore, if anyone—which may God forbid— should wilfully dare to deny or call in doubt what has been defined by us, let him know that he certainly has abandoned the divine and catholic faith.

A further development can be found in chapter 8 of the document of Vatican II entitled *Dogmatic Constitution on the Church*. Here Mary is seen "not merely as passively engaged by God, but as freely cooperating in the work of man's salvation through faith and obedience." She is the "mother to us in the order of grace."

> The predestination of the Blessed Virgin as Mother of God was associated with the incarnation of the divine word: in the designs of divine Providence she was the gracious mother of the divine Redeemer here on earth, and above all others and in a singular way the generous associate and humble handmaid of the Lord. She conceived, brought forth, and nourished Christ, she presented him to the Father in the temple, shared her Son's sufferings as he died on the cross. Thus, in a wholly singular way she co-operated by her obedience, faith, hope and burning charity in the work of the Saviour in restoring supernatural life to souls. For this reason she is a mother to us in the order of grace.
>
> The motherhood of Mary in the order of grace continues uninterruptedly from the consent which she loyally gave at the Annunciation and which she sustained without wavering beneath the cross, until the eternal fulfilment of all the elect. Taken up to heaven she did not lay aside this saving office but by her manifold intercession continues to bring us the gifts of eternal salvation. By her maternal charity, she cares for the brethren of her Son, who still journey on earth surrounded by dangers and difficulties, until they are led into their blessed home. Therefore the Blessed Virgin is invoked in the Church

under the titles of Advocate, Helper, Benefactress, and Mediatrix. This, however, is so understood that it neither takes away anything from nor adds anything to the dignity and efficacy of Christ the one Mediator.

John Paul II, in his encyclical *Redemptor Hominis*, included a last chapter entitled "The Mother in Whom We Trust." In it Mary, as the mother of the church, is given a prominent place in the history of salvation. It is said that when Jesus was raised on the cross

her Son explicitly extended His Mother's maternity in a way that could be easily understood by every soul and every heart by designating, when He was raised on the cross, His beloved disciple as her son. . . . Later, all the generations of disciples, of those who confess and love Christ, like the apostle John, spiritually took this Mother to their own homes, and she was thus included in the history of salvation and in the Church's mission from the very beginning, that is from the moment of the Annunciation. Accordingly, we who form today's generation of disciples of Christ all wish to unite ourselves with her in a special way. . . . We believe that nobody else can bring us as Mary can into the divine and human dimension of this mystery. Nobody has been brought into it by God Himself as Mary has. It is in this that the exceptional character of the grace of the divine Motherhood consists. Not only is the dignity of this Motherhood unique and unrepeatable in the history of the human race, but Mary's participation, due to this maternity, in God's plan for man's salvation through the mystery of the Redemption is also unique in profundity and range of action.

We can say that the mystery of the Redemption
took shape beneath the heart of the Virgin of Naz-
areth when she pronounced her "fiat." From then
on, under the special influence of the Holy Spirit,
this heart, the heart of both a virgin and a mother,
has always followed the work of her Son and has
gone out to all those whom Christ has embraced and
continues to embrace with inexhaustible love. For
that reason her heart must also have the inexhaus-
tibility of a mother. The special characteristic of the
motherly love that the Mother of God inserts in the
mystery of the Redemption and the life of the Church
finds expression in its exceptional closeness to man
and all that happens to him. It is in this that the
mystery of the Mother consists (*Redemptor Hominis*.
Printed in the USA by the Daughters of St. Paul,
Boston, Mass. [Vatican translation from Vatican Po-
lyglot Press], pp. 56, 57).

To be sure, Mary, the mother of Jesus, also has a
definite place in the hearts and minds of evangelicals.
Their high regard for her is based on the Gospel nar-
ratives concerning her place in Jesus' earthly ministry and in the early church as recorded in the Book
of Acts. However, the dogmatic affirmations of her
immaculate conception, her perpetual virginity, and
her assumption into heaven in bodily form lack biblical foundation. Nor is there biblical basis for titles
such as "Queen of Heaven," "Mother of the Church,"
and "Queen of all Saints," nor for the belief that she
constantly intercedes in behalf of believers.

The last half of the present century has witnessed
renewed efforts in many ways by the Roman Catholic
Church to assert Mary's uniqueness. From the time
of the dogmatic declaration in 1950 of her bodily

assumption into heaven until the present, Mary has been made the object of intensive studies in Roman Catholic theological circles. Much has been said about her function as Mediatrix, with all the consequent connotations of the term. In the Vatican document, *Marialis Cultus*, produced under the papacy of Paul VI, the centrality of Mary's person for the different seasons of the liturgical year is so emphasized that even Christmas appears to center on Mary rather than on Jesus Christ.[1] Paul VI's *Evangelii Nuntiandi* accords her a prominent role in the whole process of evangelization, and calls her "the morning star of evangelization." From a similar perspective, the bishops of Mexico issued a pastoral letter in 1984 calling attention to Mary of Guadalupe's place in the history of evangelization in that country, as contributing primarily to the formation of Mexican identity

1. "In the revised ordering of the Christmas period it seems to us that the attention of all should be directed towards the restored Solemnity of Mary the holy Mother of God. This celebration, placed on January 1 in conformity with the ancient indication of the liturgy of the City of Rome, is meant to commemorate the part played by Mary in this mystery of salvation. It is meant also to exalt the singular dignity which this mystery brings to the 'holy Mother . . . through whom we were found worthy to receive the Author of this life'. It is likewise a fitting occasion for renewing adoration for the newborn Prince of Peace, for listening once more to the glad tidings of the angels (cf. Lk. 2:14), and for imploring from God, through the Queen of Peace, the supreme gift of peace" (Apostolic exhortation of Pope Paul VI, "For the Right Ordering and Development of Devotion to the Blessed Virgin Mary—*Marialis Cultis*," February 2, 1974. [Printed by Daughters of St. Paul, Boston, Mass.; taken from *L'Osservatore Romano*, English weekly edition, April 4, 1974, official Vatican translation]).

and to the Mexican sense of self-determination. In
the light of current trends to rediscover the ministry
of the Holy Spirit, Mary's contribution in that ministry has been reiterated to the point where she is
called "the Spouse of the Holy Spirit." For "it was
with her, in her, and of her that He [the Holy Spirit]
produced His Masterpiece which is a God made man.
"The Substantial Love of the Father and the Son has
espoused Mary, in order to produce Jesus Christ."[2]

Perhaps the greatest impetus for this Marian devotion—in confirmation of the many dogmas and
theological assertions—has been given recently during the papacy of John Paul II, particularly in predominantly Roman Catholic countries. His visits to
the shrines of Guadalupe in Mexico, the Black Madonna in Poland, and the Virgin of Lourdes in France
were not simply pilgrimages of a devoted soul, but
occasions for pontifical pronouncements to exalt the
qualities of a virgin as well as her participation in
the whole salvific plan of God. Mary of Guadalupe,
of Poland, of Lourdes, as well as of many other places
throughout the world, are all the mother of the eternal, incarnate Word. In John Paul II's words: "[Mary],
you are the woman promised in Eden, the woman
chosen from eternity to be the Mother of the Word,
the Mother of divine Wisdom, the Mother of the Son
of God. Hail, Mother of God!"[3]

2. Patrick Gaffney, S.M.M., *Mary's Spiritual Maternity According to St. Louis de Montfort* (Bay Shore, N.Y.: Montfort, 1976),
38–49.

3. Pope John Paul II, "Homily at the Basilica of Guadalupe,"
in *Puebla and Beyond*, ed. John Eagleson and Philip Scharper,
trans. John Drury (Maryknoll, N.Y.: Orbis, 1979), 72.

As evangelicals we consider the Roman Catholic doctrines concerning Mary a formidable barrier between ourselves and Roman Catholics. Moreover, the many syncretistic practices associated with Mary in different parts of the world, particularly in countries of Latin Europe, Latin America, and the Philippines, are abominations to an evangelical conscience. We join the author of old in saying: "The mother of Jesus is not the papal Mary."

We as evangelical Christians are deeply offended by Rome's Marian dogmas because they cast a shadow upon the sufficiency of the intercession of Jesus Christ, lack all support from Scripture, and detract from the worship that Christ alone deserves.

This was the position of the Reformers in the sixteenth century.[4] It is still the evangelical position today. "If anybody does sin, we have one who speaks to the Father in our defense—Jesus Christ, the Righteous One" (1 John 2:1 NIV).

---

4. The Ten Theses of Berne (1528) openly claimed that, since Christ is the only Mediator and Advocate between God the Father and believers, to invoke other mediators and advocates is contrary to Scripture. The Geneva Confession rejected the intercession of saints as a superstition invented by men (XII). The Augsburg Confession states that the Scripture teaches "not to invoke saints, or to ask help of saints, because [Scripture] propounds unto us one Christ the Mediator, Propitiatory, High-Priest, and Intercessor" (XXI).

4

Authority in the Church

We as evangelicals confess the supreme authority of the Holy Scriptures for all matters of faith and conduct. As paragraph 2 of the Lausanne Covenant (1974) states:

We affirm the divine inspiration, truthfulness and authority of both Old and New Testament scriptures in their entirety as the only written word of God, without error in all that it affirms, and the only infallible rule of faith and practice. We also affirm the power of God's word to accomplish his purpose of salvation. The message of the Bible is addressed to all mankind. For God's revelation in Christ and in Scripture is unchangeable. Through it the Holy Spirit still speaks today. He illumines the minds of God's people in every culture to perceive its truth freshly through their own eyes, and thus discloses to the whole church ever more of the many-coloured wisdom of God. (2 Tim. 3:16; 2 Pet. 1:21; John 10:35; Isa. 55:11; 1 Cor. 1:21; Rom. 1:16; Matt. 5:17, 18; Jude 3; Eph. 1:17, 18; 3:10, 18).

Most of our churches accept creeds and confessions in which they elaborate their perception of biblical truth as well as rules and regulations for its application to life. "But these are themselves subordinate to Scripture, and being the composition of men are fallible documents," comments John R. W. Stott. He adds: "There is only one supreme and infallible rule which determines the beliefs and practices of the church and that is Scripture itself. To this we may always appeal even from the confessions, traditions and conventions of a church."[1]

As evangelicals we understand that our position is in conflict with the Roman Catholic acceptance of tradition and the so-called living voice of the church as sources of revelation and authority alongside of the Scriptures. To such acceptance we attribute the development of dogmas contrary to what we see as explicit and consistent teaching of Scripture. To it we also attribute the past neglect of the Bible in the daily life of the Roman church, especially in countries where it was predominant. By contrast, evangelical church life and missionary activity is characterized by the translation, distribution, and proclamation of the message of the Bible. We as evangelicals have always accepted the study of the text of Scripture as the centerpiece of theological education and theological work. We therefore now welcome all recent signs of renewed interest in the Bible in Roman Catholic circles.

Vatican II offers evidence of the degree to which biblical movements have been spreading within the

1. John R. W. Stott, in *The New Face of Evangelicalism: An International Symposium on the Lausanne Covenant*, ed. C. René Padilla (Downers Grove: Inter-Varsity, 1976), 37–38.

Roman Catholic Church. This is demonstrated by the following paragraphs from the *Dogmatic Constitution on Divine Revelation:*

> Easy access to sacred Scripture should be provided for all the Christian faithful. . . . And if, given the opportunity and the approval of Church authority, these translations are produced in cooperation with the separated brethren as well, all Christians will be able to use them (22).
>
> Sacred theology rests on the written word of God together with sacred tradition, as its primary and perpetual foundation. By scrutinizing in the light of faith all truth stored up in the mystery of Christ, theology is most powerfully strengthened and constantly rejuvenated by that word. For the sacred Scriptures contain the word of God, and, since they are inspired, really are the word of God; and so the study of the sacred page is, as it were, the soul of sacred theology. By the same word of Scripture the ministry of the word also takes wholesome nourishment and yields fruits of holiness. This ministry includes pastoral preaching, catechetics, and all other Christian instruction, among which the liturgical homily should have an exceptional place (24).

This biblical movement started in the Roman church long before Vatican II. Its rise is evident in the following historic milestones: the Biblical School of Jerusalem and the *Revue Biblique* (1892), the Pontifical Bible Institute (1909), the German Catholic Work for the Bible (1933), and the three great encyclicals on biblical matters: *Providentissimus Deus* by Leo XIII (1893), *Spiritus Paraclitus* by Benedict XV (1920), and *Divino Afflante Spiritu* by Pius XII (1943).

Today we cannot deny the abundant biblical references in contemporary papal documents, the multi-
plication of Catholic translations of the Bible in
Spanish, Portuguese, French, and Italian, and the
development of a formidable array of Roman Catholic Bible scholarship in countries where formerly
the Bible had little place. It is evident that Roman
Catholics are now ready to invest a great amount of
human and financial resources into the publication
of biblical materials.

Does Vatican II represent a change in the traditional Catholic way of understanding the authority
of the Bible? It is public knowledge that the *Constitution on Divine Revelation* was one of the most de-
bated documents during the council. An evangelical
observer there refers to it as "an unusually tension-
filled debate"[2] between those who defended the idea
of two sources of revelation and those who proposed
a new understanding of the question. The final document shows certain changes from the position of
the councils of Trent and Vatican I:

> Christ the Lord, in whom the full revelation of the
> supreme God is brought to completion (cf. 2 Cor.
> 1:20; 3:16; 4:6), commissioned the apostles to preach
> to all men that gospel which is the source of all
> saving truth and moral teaching and thus to impart
> to them divine gifts. . . . But in order to keep the
> gospel forever whole and alive within the Church,
> the apostles left bishops as their successors, "hand-

2. G. C. Berkouwer, *The Second Vatican Council and the New
Catholicism* (Grand Rapids: Eerdmans, 1965), 89.

ing over their own teaching role" to them. This sacred tradition, therefore, and sacred Scripture of both the Old and the New Testament are like a mirror in which the pilgrim church on earth looks at God, from whom she has received everything, until she is brought finally to see Him as He is face to face (cf. 1 John 3:2) (7).

This tradition which comes from the apostles develops in the Church with the help of the Holy Spirit. For there is a growth in the understanding of the realities and the words which have been handed down (8).

Hence there exists a close connection and communication between sacred tradition and sacred Scripture. For both of them, flowing from the same divine wellspring, in a certain way merge into a unity and tend toward the same end. For sacred Scripture is the word of God inasmuch as it is consigned to writing under the inspiration of the divine Spirit. To the successors of the apostles, sacred tradition hands on in its full purity God's word which was entrusted to the apostles by Christ the Lord and the Holy Spirit. Thus, led by the light of the Spirit of truth, these successors can in their preaching preserve this word of God faithfully, explain it, and make it more widely known. Consequently it is not from sacred Scripture alone that the Church draws her certainty about everything which has been revealed. Therefore both sacred tradition and sacred Scripture are to be accepted and venerated with the same sense of devotion and reverence (9).

Vatican II avoided affirming two sources of revelation. Rather, consistent with the Roman Catholic Church's self-understanding, the council connected

Scripture and tradition, together with the magisterium, as coming from a single source of revelation. This view is clearly formulated as follows: "It is clear therefore, that sacred tradition, sacred Scripture and the teaching authority of the Church, in accord with God's most wise design, are so linked and joined together, that one cannot stand without the others, and that all together and each in its own way under the action of the one Holy Spirit contribute effectively to the salvation of souls" (10).

The document shows a church that is now more open to Scripture in daily life and in theology. But when it comes to the question of authority, the Roman church still reserves to herself as an institution a power that according to official teaching is subordinate to Scripture (10), but which in practice is superior to it in the final instance. This position is based upon the role of the church in the process of the transmission of Scripture. Consequently we must still affirm, with the Reformers of the sixteenth century, the unique authority of Scripture. The words of Calvin are clear and relevant:

> Paul testifies that the Church "is built on the foundation of the apostles and the prophets" (Eph. 2:20). If the doctrine of the apostles and prophets is the foundation of the Church, the former must have had its certainty before the latter began to exist. . . . Nothing therefore can be more absurd than the fiction that the power of judging Scripture is in the Church, and that on her nod its certainty depends. When the Church receives it and gives it the stamp of her authority, she does not make that authentic

which was otherwise doubtful or controverted, but
acknowledging it as the truth of God, she as in duty
bound, shows her reverence by an unhesitating assent (*Institutes*, 1.7.2).

Good evangelical theology recognizes that the
Spirit judges and corrects both the traditions and the
teaching authority of the church on the basis of
Scripture. Though the *Constitution on Divine Revelation* makes room for Scripture in Roman Catholic
life in a way that contrasts with Trent and Vatican I,
it is still clearly different from the principle of *sola
Scriptura*.

The new presence and use of the Bible in Catholic
life challenges us to reconsider the serious question
of the interpretation of Scripture. This brings the her-
meneutical problem to the fore in theological debate.
We must acknowledge that often we have also set our
evangelical traditions above Scripture. In many in-
stances our lip service to biblical authority con-
tradicts the predominant place we give to our
denominational and historical baggage. In many
missionary situations the culture of the missionary
has often been imposed upon our understanding of
God's Word. The time has come for evangelicals
around the world to work together on a contextual
hermeneutics that will benefit from the rich expres-
sions of evangelical faith that are now taking root in
so many nations and cultures. In this task we should
never forget that for the Reformers the authority of
the Bible in our lives is inseparable from the witness
of the Holy Spirit: "For as God alone can properly
bear witness to his own words, so these words will
not obtain full credit in the hearts of men until they

are sealed by the inward testimony of the Spirit. The same Spirit, therefore, who spoke by the mouth of the prophets, must penetrate in our hearts, in order to convince us that they faithfully delivered the message with which they were divinely entrusted" (Calvin, *Institutes*, 1.7.4).

As evangelicals we are also concerned that Roman Catholic scholarship has not taken adequate account of developments in biblical studies within the evangelical world over the past three decades. Meanwhile, Catholic scholarship continues to assimilate and accept liberal and neo-liberal Protestant ideas that evangelical faith feels compelled to reject. Such Roman Catholic neglect of evangelical thought can be attributed in part to our own isolation, which itself stems from a misunderstanding of the biblical concept of separation and from reservations about the ecumenical movement. Yet a body of biblical scholarship has emerged from evangelical circles that invites Roman Catholic attention.

As evangelicals we should not be closed to the power of God's Spirit and God's Word operating in the lives of people within the Roman Catholic Church. Though Roman Catholic dogma closes the way to truly biblical reformation, we should not underestimate the results of Scripture reading and application at every level of Roman Catholic life. The best way to face this Catholicism-in-ferment is by a renewed commitment to and understanding of our evangelical position, thus turning an attentive ear to God's Word and God's Spirit for our own reformation. In that strength we need not fear dialogue or confrontation.

5

The Pope and Infallibility

Evangelical reflection on Roman Catholicism cannot ignore the institution of the papacy and its claim to infallibility. For even if the inadequacy of other Roman Catholic doctrines were exposed, but papal infallibility were left untouched, Roman Catholicism could then still sustain its convictions on those other doctrines by an appeal to the authority of the pope.

The question of papal infallibility therefore continues to hold the attention of both Roman Catholics and Protestants. It seems that the papacy is losing credit among some Roman Catholic thinkers. At the same time, however, certain ecclesial circles outside the Roman Catholic Church are showing a growing interest in it. There is good reason, therefore, to review some of the characteristic elements of Roman Catholic teaching on the papacy.

According to Roman Catholic dogma, authority was conferred by Christ upon the apostles, Peter being the prince of the apostles, and from the apostles upon the bishops in an unbroken line of apostolic succession, provided the bishops remain in communion with the Roman pontiffs as successors of Peter. The first

Vatican Council of 1870, after stating clearly that the doctrine of the primacy of the pope had been professed by the church from the very beginning, declares that when the pope speaks *ex cathedra* in matters of faith and morals, he is gifted with infallibility. His decisions are therefore "unchangeable in themselves and not because of the consent of the church" (Session 4.4; Denzinger, 3073–75).

Despite attempts by some to offer a qualified interpretation of this pronouncement, the principle of papal infallibility continues unchanged as Roman Catholic dogma. This remains so, even though the Second Vatican Council made provision for a college of bishops to assist the pope (*De Ecclesia*, 22–26). For collegiality is always to be interpreted in the light of papal primacy. The pope holds the supreme office. He embodies magisterial authority over the entire life of the Roman Catholic Church. This dogma, formulated definitively by Vatican I, is reaffirmed forcefully in the documents of Vatican II in the following words:

> The college or body of bishops has no authority unless it is simultaneously conceived of in terms of its head, the Roman Pontiff, Peter's successor, and without any lessening of his power of primacy over all, pastors as well as the general faithful. For in virtue of his office, that is, as Vicar of Christ and pastor of the whole Church, the Roman Pontiff has full, supreme, and universal power over the Church. And he can always exercise this power freely (*De Ecclesia*, 22).

This magisterial authority extends to the entire episcopal order of the Roman Catholic Church.

> [For] the order of bishops is the successor to the college of the apostles in teaching authority and pastoral rule; or, rather, in the episcopal order the apostolic body continues without a break. Together with its head, the Roman Pontiff, and never without this head, the episcopal order is the subject of supreme and full power over the universal Church. But this power can be exercised only with the consent of the Roman Pontiff (*De Ecclesia*, 22).

Vatican II adds that "the infallibility promised to the Church resides also in the body of bishops when that body exercises supreme teaching authority with the successor of Peter. To the resultant definitions the assent of the Church can never be wanting" (*De Ecclesia*, 25).

The extent of papal infallibility claimed by the Roman church is clear from the statement that "thus religious submission of will and mind must be shown in a special way to the authentic teaching authority of the Roman Pontiff, even when he is not speaking *ex cathedra*" (*De Ecclesia*, 25).

Already in the nineteenth century critical discussion within the Roman Catholic Church centered on the primacy and infallibility of the pope, with strong objections being raised against these doctrines. Continuing rigorous historical studies have clearly indicated the many definitely nontheological factors involved in the First Vatican Council's declaration of the dogma on papal infallibility (suppression of freedom, composition of the commissions, siege mentality, material interests, political pressures, etc.).[1] Such studies have brought to light the problematic character and serious implications of that decision.

As part of the strong reaction in modern society against all authority structures, sociological critiques have also been directed against papal authority. Such critiques reject the idea of papal infallibility because of its authoritarian premises. They call into question all authority structures. Our misgivings concerning the papacy do not rely upon such arguments, in view of the basic anarchistic spirit that inspires them.

More significant for evangelicals is the larger theological background that forms the context for the pronouncement on papal infallibility. This dogma is a final consequence of the infallibility that is attributed to the Church of Rome itself. If the Church of Rome were indeed infallible and as such prior and superior to Scripture, its appeal to Scripture would be devoid of real significance.

Taking issue with this view, Luther already placed the Roman Catholic position on the same level as the

1. Cf. August Bernhard Hasler, *Pius IX (1846–1878), päpstliche Unfehlbarkeit und 1. Vatikanisches Konzil: Dogmatisierung und Durchsetzung einer Ideologie*, 2 vols. (Stuttgart: Hiersemann, 1977), xvii–627; idem, *Wie der Papst unfehlbar wurde: Macht und Ohnmacht eines Dogmas* [München: Piper, 1977, 1980 (Italian trans., Torino, 1982)]. Typical of such reaction is the Keenan Catechism, in use in the Roman Catholic Church until 1870 and carrying its official stamp of approval. It attributed the idea of papal infallibility to Protestant inventions, and therefore categorically rejected it. Even after 1870 this catechism continued to be published without substantial change, except for the sentence in question.

doctrine of the "Enthusiasts," since in both cases the claimed possession of the Holy Spirit implies an independence from the Word of God.[2] For evangelical faith, however, it is not the church that gives birth to the Word, but the Word that gives birth to the church (1 Pet. 1:23; James 1:18). We have but one Master, whose infallible teaching is contained once and for all in the Scriptures. Listening to and obeying that Word, we hear the message of the one and only Lord.

Scripture leaves no room for mere corrections on the Roman Catholic doctrine of the papacy. It compels us instead to reject the very idea of Petrine primacy as the basis for papal infallibility. The New Testament is not concerned to elevate Peter above the other apostles, nor to institute an enduring "office of Peter"; nor did Peter himself ever suggest it (1 Pet. 5:1–4). Truth and unity are far better served by the confession of the unique lordship of Jesus Christ than in any other way. Under the kingship of Jesus Christ as the sole and supreme Head of the church, we as evangelicals therefore seek to honor the subservient role of God's people in the governance of the church through their exercise of the office of all believers.

The papacy, with its claim to infallibility, stands in the way of renewal within Roman Catholicism. It also poses an immense obstacle to Christian unity. It prevents, moreover, an obedient listening to the voice of the one true Lord of the church. The doctrine

2. Martin Luther, "Vorlesungen über Mose," in *D. Martin Luthers Werke* (Weimarer Ausgabe, 1911), vol. 42, p. 334, line 12.

of papal infallibility is therefore not a "divinely revealed dogma"[3] that "all Christians must believe."[4]
It is rather an idea that no Christian can accept without denying the teachings of the infallible Scriptures.

---

3. H. Denzinger and A. Schönmetzer, *Enchiridion Symbolorum*, no. 3073 (Freiburg im Breisgau: Herder, 1965).
4. Ibid., no. 3059–60.

6

Modernism and Theological Liberalism

Both of these concepts, "liberalism" as well as "modernism," are difficult to define clearly. This holds true of contemporary Roman Catholicism no less than of contemporary Protestantism. Yet together these two concepts do reflect to a large degree the crisis of twentieth-century Christendom—within Roman Catholic as well as Protestant churches. The term *modernism* indicates that we are dealing with issues born of the post-Enlightenment "modern mind." By "liberalism" we mean that widespread movement during the past two centuries that is known more precisely as "theological liberalism." It calls into question fundamental articles of the historic Christian faith.

From the decrees of its latest councils (1869–70 and 1962–65) and its many papal encyclicals over the past century, the Roman Catholic Church has clearly identified what it understands by the threat of modernist/liberalist heresies within its circles—

which parallel closely positions held by some outside of Roman Catholic circles and which we as evangelicals would also regard as heretical. These include attacks upon such biblically based doctrines as the inspiration, authority, and infallibility of Scripture; the deity of Christ; the virgin birth; the reality of miracles; the bodily resurrection and ascension of Jesus Christ; the doctrines of creation, original sin, and the last things; together with major aspects of Christian ethics. Modernism/liberalism also launched assaults upon typically Roman Catholic traditions, such as papal infallibility, the immaculate conception and heavenly assumption of the virgin Mary, celibate clergy, the exclusion of women from priestly ordination, and the denunciation of artificial birth-control methods. Our concern at this point is with the former catalogue of errors.

Such modernist/liberalist intrusions into the thought and life of the church are traceable to the radical and sweeping impact of the eighteenth-century Enlightenment. By the middle of the nineteenth century this movement had created a major crisis within the Roman Catholic Church. The hierarchy viewed the church as a fortress under siege. One after another, bishops of Rome such as Pius IX, Leo XIII, Pius X, and Pius XII took vigorous steps to stem the modernist/liberalist tide and to maintain and restore both biblical and traditional orthodoxy. This is evident from the papal declaration of the immaculate conception in 1854, the publication of the syllabus of errors in 1864, the pronouncement on papal infallibility by Vatican I in 1870, the elevation of Thomas

Aquinas to patron saint of educators and angelic doc-
tor of the church in 1879, the series of papal encyclicals late in the nineteenth century condemning
liberal ideologies and modern culture, the denunciation of theological modernism in 1907, the imposi-
tion of the anti-modernist oath upon all priests in
1910, the repeated affirmations of Thomism as the
trusted source of Roman Catholic teaching during
the early decades of this century, climaxed finally in
the encyclical *Humani Generis*, and the papal declaration on the heavenly assumption in 1950.[1]

Meanwhile, during the years preceding and following World War II the "New Theology" emerged upon
the scene. The papacy responded by issuing stern
though generally vague warnings against "certain
false opinions" being promulgated by this school of
thought: its reliance upon existentialist philosophy,
its acceptance of the historical-critical method in
biblical studies, and its tendency to reevaluate crit-
ically the development of dogma within church tradition. Rome apparently sensed in the rise of this
"New Theology" a disguised return to the "old modernism." This was vigorously denied by its advocates
and defenders. To others, however, as time went by,
the connections seemed too obvious to be overlooked:
the "New Theology" is in effect an updated revision
on the "old modernism." Add to that the momentum
of the "aggiornamento" spirit unleashed by
John XXIII, the "renewals" enacted by Vatican II, and
the confusing developments of the past two de-

1. Cf. William Challis, "Biblical Studies and Roman Catholicism," *Churchman* 94 (1980): 323.

cades—it is then understandable that many Roman Catholics are left in a state of "spiritual dizziness." The doors and windows of the Church of Rome now stand wide open to radically new ideas. Its largely monolithic confessional and theological structure (*semper eadem*) is crumbling. The philosophies of Hegel, Marx, and Heidegger are making their deep inroads. Post-Barthian and post-Bultmannian theologies, together with the monist ideas of process theologians, are prevalent in Roman Catholic as well as in mainline Protestant circles. The basic thrust in the writings of Roman Catholic thinkers such as Rahner, Teilhard de Chardin, Küng, Schillebeeckx, and Schoonenberg do not differ substantially from those of their secular Protestant counterparts. The granting of a *Nihil Obstat* and an *Imprimatur* seems until recently to have been little more than a routine ritual. Along the way Roman conservatives may have won some battles against modernism/liberalism. But now, despite continuing papal resistance, is Rome losing the war? Will the "new freedom"—the Enlightenment revisited—win the day?

Clearly Rome is not immune to modernist/liberalist infiltrations. What accounts for this growing openness to alien ideas? We cannot overlook Roman Catholicism's long-standing commitment to a dualist nature/grace world view. With it comes a strong internal tension between authority and freedom, based on the dogma of two orders of reality and correspondingly two orders of knowledge. In the higher realm of faith, grace, and supernatural things, the teaching office of the church exercises its dogmatic authority firmly in disciplining departures from re-

vealed truth. But in the lower realm of nature, where
the natural and social sciences, scientific data, and
philosophical studies prevail, Rome's magisterial
policy allows ample room for free rational inquiry.

This dichotomy raises a number of critical questions. Where does the line of demarcation lie between
these two areas of jurisdiction? Who draws the line?
How can the limits of academic freedom be circum-
scribed? Theoretically this dichotomy defies clear
definition. In practice too this "upstairs/downstairs"
distinction between grace and nature is untenable,
for eventually nature "eats up" grace (Francis
Schaeffer). Within the cultural dynamics of our age,
reason overwhelms faith. Rationality reshapes traditional Roman Catholic fidelity to the body of basic
Christian beliefs. Adherence to the modern mind
presses the articles of Christian faith into its own
mold. The magisterial authority of the Roman church
then finds it increasingly difficult to hold the line
against the aggressive claims made in behalf of academic freedom—especially in the face of the secular
spirit of our times. Current debates concerning lib-
eration theologies amply illustrate this dilemma. Thus
natural theology renders a theology of grace increasingly irrelevant.

While critizing these heresies within Roman Catholicism, we as evangelical Christians, facing the
complexities of our modern world, and conscious of
similar shortcomings in our own tradition, reaffirm
our commitment to a biblically unified world view
and to the fundamental articles of the historic Christian faith.

7

Justification
by Faith Alone

Paul's letter to Roman Christians has played a central role in nearly every reformation in the life of the church. This is understandable, given man's persistent inclination toward self-help patterns of religion. Romans stands as a frontal challenge to all such forms of self-righteousness. Its central teaching is justification by faith alone. This is the heart of the gospel. Luther therefore calls Romans "the most important document in the New Testament, the gospel in its purest expression: . . . in essence it is a brilliant light, almost enough to illumine the whole Bible" (preface to *Romans*).

For the Reformers, justification by faith was more than merely one doctrine among others. It is the very foundation of the assurance of salvation and the life of sanctification. Calvin calls it "the main hinge on which religion turns" (*Institutes*, 3.11.1). From Reformation times to the present the doctrine of justification by faith alone has repeatedly emerged as the crucial point of confrontation between Roman Catholics and evangelicals. Even in our ecumenical age it has lost little of its deeply religious urgency. Perhaps a hasty survey will help to keep the issue clearly in focus.

Tirelessly Martin Luther proclaimed the biblical message that "the just shall live by faith alone." Consistent with his views on law and gospel, Luther's stance is clear: "The promises of God give what the commandments of God demand, and fulfil what the law prescribes, so that all things may be God's alone, both the commandments and the fulfilling of the commandments. He alone commands, he alone fulfills." Therefore "no good work can rely upon the Word of God or live in the soul, for faith alone and the Word of God rule in the soul." It is clear then, Luther adds, "that a Christian has all he needs in faith and needs no works to justify him" (*The Freedom of the Christian*): he receives a righteousness that is not his own, but a *justitia aliena* (an "alien righteousness"), a free gift of God's grace.

Similarly, a second-generation Reformer, John Calvin, holds that he is justified who, "excluded from the righteousness of works, grasps the righteousness of Christ through faith, and clothed in it, appears in God's sight not as a sinner, but as a righteous man." Our justification by faith therefore means "nothing else than to acquit of guilt him who was accused, as if his innocence were confirmed. . . . Since God justifies us by the intercession of Christ, he absolves us not only by the confirmation of our innocence but by the imputation of righteousness, so that we who are not righteous in ourselves may be reckoned as such in Christ" (*Institutes*, 3.11.2–3). Thus Calvin reaf-

firms Luther's teaching on the "great challenge"—
Christ became what he was not, unrighteous, to make
us what we by nature are not, righteous. All this is
sola gratia and *sola fide*.

It was in vigorous response to this newly rearticulated proclamation of the gospel that the Council
of Trent formulated its dogmas. Its decrees still stand
as the official confessional voice of the Counter Reformation. Modern Catholicism is compelled to take
the irrevocable teachings of Trent on justification by
faith as its starting point in the renewed contemporary dialogues. Recognizing that often affirmations
are best clarified by their accompanying rejections,
current encounters between Roman Catholics and
evangelicals must come to terms with (at least) the
following four "canons concerning justification."

9. If anyone shall say that the sinner is justified by
faith alone, meaning that nothing else is required to
cooperate in order to obtain the grace of justification, and that it is not in any way necessary that he
be prepared and disposed by the action of his own
will—let him be anathema (Denzinger, 1559).

11. If anyone shall say that men are justified either
by the sole imputation of the righteousness of Christ
or by the sole remission of sins, to the exclusion of
the grace and charity that is poured forth in their
hearts by the Holy Spirit and remains in them, or
also that the grace by which we are justified is only
the good will of God—let him be anathema (Denzinger, 1561).

12. If anyone shall say that justifying faith is nothing else but confidence [*fiducia*] in divine mercy,

which remits sins for Christ's sake, or that it is this
confidence alone which justifies us—let him be
anathema (Denzinger, 1562).

24. If anyone shall say that the justice [righteous-
ness] received is not preserved and also increased
before God through good works, but that those works
are merely the fruits and signs of justification obtained, but not the cause of its increase—let him be
anathema (Denzinger, 1574).

In recent times, however, the Reformers' ringing
affirmation of justification by faith alone has gained
a more appreciative hearing even in Roman Catholic
circles. We are witnessing a new openness to this central biblical teaching.

Around the middle of this century, for example,
the longstanding Trentine dogmas became the focal
point of renewed theological reflection. Hans Küng
forced the issue with his book *Justification* (1957).
Launching a "self-appraisal" of his Roman Catholic
tradition, and reassessing it "in the mirror of Karl
Barth's theology," Küng argues that we are labor-
ing under a five-hundred-year-old misunderstanding.
Rightly understood, he contends, the views of Trent
and of the Reformers on justification by faith are in
essential agreement.

Küng's book includes an introductory letter of response by Karl Barth, who offers the following amaz-
ing and amusing rejoinder:

> You can imagine my considerable amazement at this
> bit of news; and I suppose that many Roman Cath-
> olic readers will at first be no less amazed. . . . Of
> course, the problem is whether what you have pre-

sented here really represents the teaching of your church. . . . If the things you cite from Scripture, from older and more recent Roman Catholic theology, from Denzinger and hence from the Tridentine text, do actually represent the teaching of your church and are establishable as such, . . . then, having twice gone to the church of Santa Maria Maggiore in Trent to commune with the genius loci, I may very well have to hasten there a third time to make contrite confession—"Fathers, I have sinned." But taking the statements of the Sixth Session as we now have them before us—statements correctly or incorrectly formulated for reasons then considered compelling—don't you agree that I should be permitted to plead mitigating circumstances for the considerable difficulty I had trying to discover in that text what you have found to be true Catholic teaching?

Though Barth's views on justification by faith differ significantly from those of the Reformers, as well as from our own, we agree with his critical conclusion, contradicting Küng, that the views of Trent stand radically opposed to those of the Reformers.

These recent and surprising developments have not yet run their full course, as is evident from current Roman Catholic/Lutheran discussions. These meetings have resulted in the publication of an interconfessional statement on justification by faith, including the following lines: "Our entire hope of justification and salvation rests on Christ Jesus and on the gospel, whereby the good news of God's merciful action in Christ is made known; we do not place our ultimate trust in anything other than God's promise and saving work in Christ" (*Origins,* October, 1983, 279). While we are inclined to subscribe to such a heart-warming statement, we confess our uneasiness with the restriction that the word "ultimate" seems to imply. We also observe that the nature of justification, whether we are *declared* righteous or *made* righteous by infused grace, is left unclarified.

From these recent developments it appears that many are struggling these days to formulate a Roman Catholic version of the *sola gratia/sola fide* gospel, so central to the Reformation. Can Rome shed itself of its legacy of human cooperation in the act of justification? The ongoing process of updating and restating old dogmas raises further questions: Are we witnessing the birth pangs of a new Roman Catholic confession on justification by faith? Is this possible, given the Roman Catholic view on infallible truth and the unchangeability of dogma? Were the doctrinal intentions of the Tridentine fathers really different from the plain sense of their words? Are the anathemas past?

Meanwhile Trent stands firm as Rome's first-line confessional pronouncement on the reformational view of justification. This includes both its dogmatic declarations and its anathemas. Vatican I did nothing to change that. Nor was justification a major point on Vatican II's agenda. The documents of Vatican II contain only oblique references to it. They break no new ground. Apart from a new Roman Catholic confession on justification by faith, Trent remains a major barrier between heirs of the Reformation and Roman Catholicism.

8

Sacramentalism and the Eucharist

For the Church of Rome, "catholicism" and "sacramentalism" go hand in hand. Both in its theology and in its practice it gives great weight to the seven rites it calls sacraments. Already in the sixteenth century the Reformers made a decisive break with this sacramental tradition. They took issue not only with the number of ceremonies that may rightly be regarded as sacraments, but also with the importance, status, and function the Roman Catholic Church attaches to them. They did so out of loyalty to the gospel and in obedience to the principle of *sola Scriptura*. Luther led the way in this as he proclaimed the message of *sola fide* (by faith alone), calling for *fiducia* (trust in the gospel promises), and in this light denouncing the Babylonian captivity of the Roman church. With even greater cogency, Zwingli and Calvin followed suit. Various Anabaptist reformers went even further, offering an alternative sacramental theology. Ever since the sixteenth century evangelical Christians have shown a distinctively reformational distrust and distaste for Roman Catholic sacramentalism.

The Roman Catholic Church views the sacraments
as efficacious signs. That is, they accomplish what
they signify: *significando causant*—in signifying
grace, they cause it to happen. This belief implies a
conjunction of two diverse elements—a convergence
of the two concepts of "sign" and "cause." Throughout the centuries Roman Catholic theology has been
striving to express clearly a proper balance or synthesis of these two elements.

On the one hand, the idea of "signification" calls
for *subjective* involvement on the part of the recipients of the sacraments. For a "sign" is meant to be
read and acted upon by those who receive it. As "sacraments of faith" these rites call for belief, or at least
the absence of any obstacle (*obex*) to grace in the
heart of the recipients. This is a condition for fruitful
participation in the sacraments and for receiving the
grace they convey. As "signs" the sacraments are also
to be distinguished from the reality to which they
refer. Thus according to Roman teaching, the Mass
remains a nonbloody sacrifice, pointing to Golgotha,
without detracting from the once-for-all sacrifice of
the cross.

On the other hand, the idea of instrumental "causality" brings with it a full emphasis upon the *objective* efficacy of the sacraments. Sacraments work *ex
opere operato*—a canonized phrase in Roman Catholic sacramentology. It means that the sacraments
are efficacious in themselves—"they work by their
own working." The effects of sacraments are not de-
pendent upon the attitude or merits of either the
priest or the recipient—contrary to the rule that holds
for all other activities. This is so because the sacra-

mental act is in essence an act of Christ himself, operating through his servant, the priest (called "another Christ").[1] In the words of Pope Paul VI: "Let no one deny that the sacraments are acts of Christ, who administers them through the agency of men. Therefore, they are holy of themselves, and owing to the virtue of Christ they confer grace to the soul as they touch the body."[2]

Lending added strength to their causal status, sacraments are said to produce a specific effect (not grace) whenever they are validly administered, even if they are not received in faith and goodwill. This is true of the "character" conferred by baptism and holy orders, as well as in the conversion of the elements in the Eucharist. The Eucharist is viewed as the "total Christ"—that is, Christ and the church. As such it is a propitiatory sacrifice for the living and the dead.[3]

Clearly, Roman Catholic theology is hard pressed to hold these two sides of the sacrament together— "signification" and "causality."[4] This is evident in the repeated resurgence of a Scotist emphasis upon

1. The priest *alter est Christus*, according to the encyclical *Ad catholic sacerdotii* (1935) (Denzinger, *Enchiridion Symbolorum*, no. 2275); another phrase, more widely used, is *in persona Christi*, cf. Maurice Vidal, "Ministre des sacrements et foi en Jésus-Christ," in the important symposium *Sacrements de Jésus-Christ*, ed. Joseph Doré (Paris: Desclée, 1983), 206ff.

2. *Mysterium fidei*, no. 38.

3. Ibid., no. 4: "the Lord immolates himself in a non-bloody manner."

4. As noted by Thomas Aquinas, *Summa theologica*, IIIa, Q. 62, art. 1, ad 1.

the objective causality of sacraments, despite the
more balanced Thomist position that the Council of
Trent appears to endorse. It is also evident in the very
subtle and complicated theory of transubstantiation.

No part of traditional Roman Catholic sacramentology has been repealed by the Vatican. In recent
years both Paul VI and John Paul II have reempha-
sized certain aspects of it. Only a few outspoken mod-
ernists within Roman Catholic circles have dissented
from what they regard as "obsolete" forms, while
still claiming to be faithful to their deepest intent.
Yet spectacular changes have taken place. This is true
in liturgical practices: one can attend masses that
outwardly differ very little from evangelical services.
It is also true currently among many who profess
allegiance to official Roman Catholic sacramental
theology. During the post-Tridentine "modern" era,
heavy emphasis was placed on the *objective* side of
the sacraments; reflecting the juridical mind of Rome,
intending thus to bolster its institutional preroga-
tives. However, with the emergence of the liturgical
renewal movement earlier in this century, which got
underway with Pius X's blessing, a new emphasis fell
upon the community's participation in the sacraments. It stressed the organic union of sacramental
commemoration with the total life and worship of
the church. It represented a rediscovery of the riches
and more flexible understanding of sacraments in the
patristic tradition. The key idea became "mystery,"
evident especially in the "mystical" sacramentology
of Dom Odo Casel. The celebration of the Eucharist
was viewed as making the past event of salvation

history present to the faithful today, after the fashion of rites in mythical religions.

Since the middle of this century a similar "representational" view of the sacraments came to the fore, closely associated with the idea of a "memorial" feast, which allegedly reflects a Hebraic outlook. The language of salvation-history became predominant—for example, the paschal theme. Personalistic categories became popular, together with an insistence on faith as the *subjective* correlative of the sacraments—the faith of the church, for example, in the case of infant baptism. Christ or the church itself was hailed as the primordial sacrament. During the sixties the idea of "symbol" became more and more popular, but with a modification of its older, more inflexible connotations. Appealing to the concept "symbol," theologians sought to erase the hard and fast distinctions between sign and reality, between spiritual and corporeal, between subjective and *objective*. Latest developments include the political radicalization of the spiritual moment of the Eucharist. The sharing of bread and wine in remembrance of a revolutionary Jesus is experienced as a motivating symbol among liberationists in their militantly prophetic struggle against social inequities and class oppression. Moreover, some uneasiness has emerged over infant baptism, mostly among members of the charismatic movement. Others draw upon the social sciences to interpret sacramental "symbol" as an expression of ritual anthropology. One leading sacramentologist defines the sacraments, furthermore, as "the symbolic language acts of the church," as "performance language acts" by which the community receives its identity, structure, and ethos.[5]

Despite these many dramatic departures from the traditional Roman Catholic doctrine of the sacraments, the official dogma remains unchallenged, that sacraments are more than "mere" signs. They are effectual operations as means of access to God.

We as evangelicals may welcome the direction that some of these changes seem to be taking. This situation within Roman Catholicism is, however, fraught with many ambiguities. Revision is so limited on crucial points and so devoid of official sanction in its bolder strokes, that, at present, no definitive response to these changes is possible. It would be possible at this point, and perhaps even relevant and helpful, to engage in a theoretical critique of traditional Roman Catholic sacramentalism, especially on the casual efficacy it attributes to these rites. We shall, however, concentrate instead on the following more biblical objections.

The causal aspect of Roman Catholic teaching on the sacraments stands in sharp disagreement with the Scriptures. This contradiction is most blatantly evident when one compares the traditional dogma of the eucharistic sacrifice with the clear statements of the Epistle to the Hebrews concerning the finality of

5. Louis-Marie Chauvet, "Le sacramentologue aux prises avec l'Eucharistie," *La Maison-Dieu* 137 (1979): 69; idem, *Du symbolique au symbole: Essai sur les sacrements* (Paris: Cerf. 1979), reviewed by Claude Geffré, *La Maison-Dieu* 142 (1980): 49–55; idem, "Sacramentaire et christologie: La liturgie, lieu de la christologie," in *Sacrements de Jesus-Christ*, ed. Joseph Doré, 213–54.

Christ's sacrifice on the cross. On the function of sacraments Roman Catholic theology can appeal only to a misguided exegesis of some Pauline and Johannine passages. It fails also to take into account the definitely antiritualistic teachings of the New Testament (Matt. 15; Rom. 14:17; 1 Cor. 1:17; 8:8; Col. 2:16–23; Heb. 9:10; 13:9–16; 1 Pet. 3:21). It drastically reverses the balanced relationship the New Testament establishes between the preached Word, faith, baptism, and the Lord's Supper. The doctrine of a special priesthood of sacramental liturgetes can hardly be harmonized with the biblical data.[6] The fashionable theory of the sacraments as "memorials," reenacting the past in the present, lacks proper foundation. We therefore concur with the noted Anglican scholar, Roger T. Beckwith, when he says:

> This pagan Greek notion has, quite incongruously, been read into the Jewish passover. . . . The theory could never have become popular except by wishful thinking on the part of those who wanted to overcome the great theological and ecumenical problems caused by the notions of bodily presence and the mass-sacrifice, conflicting as they do with the once-for-all finality of Calvary. . . .[7]

The *objective* efficacy that Rome attributes to the sacraments, even though it is called "instrumental" and "applicatory," implies an intolerable addition to

6. As perceived by the modernist Edward Schillebeeckx, *Kerkelijk ambt* (Bloemendaal: Nelissen, 1980).
7. "The Ecumenical Quest for Agreement in Faith," *Themelios* 10 (1984): 29.

the finished work of Jesus Christ. He has fully accomplished the entire "objective" side of our salvation.
No further sacrifice is needed. The sacraments as
works of human merit, which must be mediated
through the church, represent a denial of justification
by faith alone and an infringement upon the sover-
eign freedom of God. In the words of Calvin, "When
I baptise, is it as if I had the Holy Spirit up my sleeve
to produce at any time? Or the body and blood of
the Lord to offer to whom I please? It would be sheer
presumption to attribute to mortal creatures what
belongs to Jesus Christ."[8]

At bottom, our evangelical critique of Roman
Catholic sacramentology points up the conflict between two opposing views of the Christian faith.
Rome sees itself as an extension of the incarnation,
thus divinizing human beings as they cooperate with
God's grace that is conferred by the church. Over
against this view stands our evangelical commitment
to the free gift of righteousness, imputed solely by
the grace of God, received by a true faith that an-
swers to God's Word, and based fully upon the once-
for-all expiation of guilt through the finished sacrifice
of the perfect Substitute, Christ Jesus. This confession is for us the gospel.

8. Sermon on Acts 1:4–5, as quoted by Ronald S. Wallace,
Calvin's Doctrine of the Word and Sacrament (Edinburgh: Oliver &
Boyd, 1953), 172.

9

The Mission
of the Church

Traditionally evangelicals have understood their mission basically in terms of evangelization. In predominantly Roman Catholic countries this meant a call to conversion and a change in church affiliation. But the holistic impact of the gospel also played a role in the mission of evangelicals, taking shape in the daily lives of people, especially among the poor. Contrastingly, Roman Catholic religion generally took the form of popular religiosity, keeping the poor from living as responsible stewards of God and making them victims of exploitation. Evangelicals frequently pointed out the close connection between a religiosity based upon a false or incomplete gospel and social exploitation.

Traditionally the Roman Catholic Church has understood her role in these countries as one of keeping within the fold those who had been baptized. Both her pastoral methodology and the use of social coercion through public institutions were used to this end. Her attitude toward non-Roman communions

was then defined in the old inquisitorial way of dealing with error. In some regions of the world isolated
cases of persecution still occur—though contrary to
the official policy of the Roman Catholic Church.

With the growth of secularism and the rise of liberal governments the Roman Catholic Church has
not been able to continue its former approach and
can no longer use social means of coercion as it once
did. This experience of disestablishment, as well as
the self-critical ferment coming after Vatican II, has
forced the Roman Catholic Church to revise her
understanding of mission in the world. In Latin
America and many other areas this has meant a new
emphasis on evangelization. This new impetus arises
from an awareness that a very small minority within
the baptized masses are really practicing Catholics.
Interest in the Bible and experiencing the liturgy in
the common language of the people has given Roman
Catholics a new awareness of some of the basic elements of the Christian faith that had previously been
taken for granted or obscured by the ritual.

At the same time a significant sector of the Roman
Catholic Church is demanding a radical shift in political alliances on the part of the church. This call
for a "preferential option for the poor" is basically a
call for the church to change its alignment from a
close relationship and cooperation with the ruling
elites to solidarity with the masses and the poor. Much
is at stake for the church in these changes. It remains
to be seen what the final outcome of the liberationist
ferment will be. Yet neither the liberationist position

nor the official Roman reactions to it can be uncritically embraced by evangelicals. What cannot be denied is the involvement of many priests and nuns in actions of sacrificial service to the poor with all the risks involved in times of social transformation. In this way the Church of Rome has revised her mission in the direction of a more prophetic and critical social role.

Evangelicals generally conceive of their mission first in terms of a call to personal faith in Christ and see their social role as a consequence of this spiritual transformation. From this perspective their evaluation of these new developments in the Roman Catholic Church tends to be negative, colored by suspicion about its motives and methods. They cannot deny, however, that when they first entered a Roman Catholic country, they themselves provided services in medicine, education, and social uplift as part of a holistic ministry. Even today entrance visas into some countries are possible for evangelicals mainly because of the holistic ministry they perform. As the Lausanne Covenant demonstrates, there is a renewed effort among evangelicals to understand their mission in a biblical and holistic way, without denying the fundamental human need for the gospel.

Besides stressing our basic commitment to announce the gospel of Jesus Christ, especially to those who have never heard it, we should also understand how to do this faithfully in places where it is only partially known. The biblical movement, the charismatic movement, and the base communities among

Roman Catholics are all new developments that should be taken into account in any evangelistic strategy for evangelicals. It will be to our loss if we minimize the possibilities that some forms of these movements bring with them for more basic changes in the Roman Catholic Church. We should also bear in mind that many independent forms of spiritual experience are possible within Roman Catholicism because of her inability even to retain in the fold those who are baptized, due largely to the lack of clergy and lay mobilization (*Puebla and Beyond*, 76–86).

In the past evangelicals have in many places been defenders of the separation of church and state, especially as it applies to education. In Roman Catholic-dominated countries this has meant the rejection of Roman Catholic-dominated educational systems. Today some evangelicals feel compelled to revise their approach because of the pervasive penetration of non-Christian ideologies into many educational systems and even to consider the possibility of cooperation with Roman Catholics in some aspects of this revision.

A very important aspect of missions has to do with the approach to other religions indigenous to areas where the gospel is introduced. It may be said without fear of contradiction that the Church of Rome views these other religions with greater favor than evangelicals generally do. In our judgment the Roman Catholic Church has at times taken over pagan customs, altering them on the surface, but incorporating them essentially unchanged into its life. It is not uncommon for Roman Catholics to speak of these pagan views and practices, which in fact often border on the occult, as "popular religiosity" and as stepping-stones to the gospel. To us as evangelicals this practice amounts to a kind of Christopaganism.[1]

Already in 1659 the Congregation for the Propagation of the Faith stated in a letter to the Roman Catholic communities in Southeast Asia:

> Never use any force whatsoever, nor employ any means of persuasion to induce those peoples to change their rites, their customs, and their manners of living, unless such be most clearly contrary to religion and to proper behaviour. What could be more absurd than to try to transplant [foreign customs] into China, France, Spain, Italy, or some other European country? It is not this which you should introduce, but the faith, which neither rejects nor destroys the ceremonies and customs of any people, when they are not intrinsically evil, but wants in every way to safeguard and consolidate them.[2]

The official view of the Roman Catholic Church concerning other religions (including traditional religions such as tribunal, animistic, and ancestral forms of worship, together with Judaism, Buddhism, Islam, and Hinduism) is formulated by Vatican II in

---

1. It is worthy of note that the Medellin Conference of Bishops in 1968 criticized this "popular religiosity," but that the Puebla Conference of 1978 reaffirmed it as a form of Christianity.

2. Massimo Marcocchi, "The Instruction of *Propaganda Fidei* to the Apostolic Vicars of East Asia (1659)," in *Colonialismo cristianesimo e culture extraeuropie* (Milan, 1981), 80.

the Decree, *Nostra Aetate* ("in our time"), in the following key statement:

> The Catholic Church rejects nothing which is true
> and holy in these religions. She looks with sincere
> respect upon those ways of conduct and of life, those
> rules and teachings which, though differing in many
> particulars from what she holds and sets forth,
> nevertheless often reflect a ray of that Truth which
> enlightens all men. Indeed, she proclaims and must
> ever proclaim Christ, "the way, the truth, and the
> life" (John 14:6), in whom men find the fullness of
> religious life, and in whom God has reconciled all
> things to Himself (cf. 2 Cor. 5:18–19).

The Roman Catholic Church holds that these other religions often reflect rays of the truth and rejects nothing in them that is true and holy (*Ad Gentes*, 2). The Roman Catholic Church therefore exhorts her sons that they "prudently and lovingly, through dialogue and collaboration with the followers of other religions, and in witness of Christian faith and life, acknowledge, preserve and promote the spiritual and moral goods found among these men, as well as the values of their society and culture" (*Ad Gentes*, 2). The position of Rome is that these religions may provide a preparation for ultimate entrance into the church, wherein salvation must be found.

In a historic event during his visit to Morocco in 1985, John Paul II addressed sixty thousand Islamic students at Casablanca. On that occasion he spoke of the differences that divide and the similarities that join Christians and Muslims. Concerning the similarities he said that "Abraham is the same model of faith in God for us, [a model] of submitting to his will and of confidence in his bounty. We believe in the same God, the only God, the living God, the God who creates the world and brings its creatures to perfection." It would appear from this papal statement that the present pope sees more than a "ray of truth" in Islam. For both Muslims and Christians are said to believe in the only living God.

How do we as evangelicals respond to Rome's teaching on other religions? We find the carefully guarded language of many of its official statements unobjectionable as they stand. We too would reject nothing that is true and holy, nor do we reject efforts at contextualization. Yet we observe that the historical application of these guidelines often allowed for syncretism with deadly pagan errors and much that was unholy. We discern in this a dangerous underestimation of the sinfulness of natural man and of the activity of the powers of darkness. We are disturbed when the Roman Catholic theologian Karl Rahner speaks of "anonymous Christianity" (as if people can belong to Christ without naming his name) and when Raymond Panikkar writes of the "Unknown Christ of Hinduism" or when others speak of a "latent kingdom" among people of other faiths. Approaches like these clearly negate the finality of Jesus Christ.

There is an incipient unbiblical universalism in Rome's view of these other religions. In 1949 the Holy Office pointed out that those who live good lives and follow the truth as they know it have "an implicit desire" for faith, which is sufficient for salvation.[3] There is then, according to the teaching of Rome, a universality of divine grace, even among those who do not know Christ. As Jadot says, there is "the divinely inspired possibility of salvation also for atheists and agnostics."[4]

What such views call for is not an outright rejection of the teachings and customs of the other religions, but dialogue and collaboration with them. At the same time the Church of Rome invites the adherents of other religions to believe the gospel.

We believe that the position of the Roman Catholic Church vis-à-vis these other religions stands in basic contradiction to the message of the gospel. Yet Rome does maintain the necessity of proclaiming the gospel. For it holds that incipient faith must be brought to fruition; the anonymous Christ must be made fully known. Since it has abandoned the biblical position, however, the Roman Catholic Church has assumed a very positive attitude toward non-Christian religions in some areas of the world and has accordingly baptized many people whose lives are still largely entangled in pagan thought and practice.

We as evangelicals take strong exception to all such ideas of a "Christ incognito," an "anonymous Christianity," a "latent kingdom," an incipient faith that

3. John L. Jadot, "The Growth in Roman Catholic Commitment to Interreligious Dialogue Since Vatican II," *Journal of Ecumenical Studies* 20 (1983): 369.

4. Ibid., 371.

is sufficient unto salvation, and a universalism that includes agnostics and atheists. For "every spirit that does not acknowledge Jesus is not from God" (1 John 4:3 NIV).

Conclusion

In our evaluation of Roman Catholicism we have endeavored to be true to the evangelical faith and honest and fair to the Church of Rome. Our submission to the Scriptures requires us to hold high the cardinal truths of the historic apostolic faith as proclaimed anew in the sixteenth-century Reformation of *sola Scriptura, sola gratia, sola fide, solo Christo,* all to the glory of God.

Standing in that faith we have encountered obstacles in Roman Catholicism as it manifests itself today that seriously impede fellowship and cooperation between evangelicals and Roman Catholics and are unsurmountable as long as there is no fundamental reformation according to the Word of God in the Church of Rome. It is our fervent prayer that such a reformation may take place. Unity and cooperation among Christians is highly desirable, but not at the expense of the fundamental evangelical truths that have been stated in this book. There is only one way. As has been said, only as we all draw closer to Christ can we draw closer to each other (Eph. 4:16). The road that beckons is not "come back to Rome," nor "come across to Wittenberg or Geneva," but "come together in Jerusalem," the historical-redemptive anchor point of the Christian faith.

We acknowledge that Roman Catholicism today is

not a monolithic body and that there are notable differences between the popular religiosity of its members and the elaborate theological explanations of its dogma. Moreover, the scarcity of priests and the loss of social control in many areas of the world allows for many things to happen at the local level, apart from hierarchical control. There is also a wide variety of national situations that account for a variety of experiences among evangelicals themselves in their contacts with Roman Catholics.

In our service of the Lord Jesus Christ and his church and in our obedience to our call to mission, especially where contacts with Roman Catholics are involved, we should keep in mind the findings of this study and the multiplicity of situations in which we live and work.

In an effort to evaluate recent developments in Roman Catholicism, we have given expression to our evangelical convictions. The times in which we live call for a renewed understanding and appreciation of our evangelical heritage. Biblical imperatives demand of us consistency of behavior in relation to the evangelical truths in our personal lives, in our churches, and in our positions in society.

We are constrained by the commission of our Lord (2 Cor. 5:18–20) and by the love of Christ (2 Cor. 5:14) to proclaim the gospel to all people, including those who are Roman Catholic.

We would like to think that this perspective on Roman Catholicism will provide the basis for a consensus among all the evangelical fellowships that constitute the World Evangelical Fellowship.

We make the prayer of the apostle Paul our prayer, "May the God who gives endurance and encouragement give you a spirit of unity among yourselves as you follow Christ Jesus, so that with one heart and mouth you may glorify the God and Father of our Lord Jesus Christ" (Rom. 15:5–6 NIV).

Appendix

John Paul II and Mary

Early in 1987, less than one year after the sixth General Assembly of the World Evangelical Fellowship (WEF) issued its statement, "A Contemporary Evangelical Perspective on Roman Catholicism," Pope John Paul II published his encyclical letter *Redemptoris Mater* (Mother of the Redeemer). This encyclical calls for an appraisal.

The question naturally arises whether, in view of the recent papal letter, the judgment of the WEF statement was perhaps too harsh. The evangelicals' statement concluded that the Roman Catholic doctrines concerning Mary are a "formidable barrier between ourselves and Roman Catholics." Catholic teaching on Mary, they said, is one of the "obstacles which seriously impede fellowship and cooperation between evangelicals and Roman Catholics and [which] are insurmountable as long as there is no fundamental reformation according to the Word of God in the Church of Rome." No one would be more pleased than evangelical Christians to find in *Redemptoris Mater* signs of such a reformation. We should therefore read the encyclical carefully and hopefully.

John Paul wrote this letter about Mary to mark the beginning of the Marian year (from Pentecost 1987 until the Feast of the Assumption of Mary, August 15, 1988). He issued it with the end of the twentieth century in view, for the year 2000 will mark the second millennium of the birth of the Savior and he considered it appropriate to precede that anniversary by a jubilee in celebration of the birth of Mary.

John Paul had two aims in writing *Redemptoris Mater*. The first was to emphasize the special promise of the mother of God in the mystery of Christ and his church (48).[1] To do this he had to build upon and advance beyond the declarations on the immaculate conception of Mary (1854) and the bodily assumption of Mary (1950). Lest anyone think that a virgin who was herself immaculately conceived and was later assumed bodily into heaven is too distant from lowly sinners to be of any good, they should be told that "the new Eve, the Mother of the Church, carries on in heaven her maternal role with regard to the members of Christ, cooperating in the birth and development of divine life in the souls of the redeemed" (47). Mary, the mother of God, is at the center of the pilgrim church.

John Paul's second aim was to present Mary as the one who can promote unity among the churches of Christendom, inasmuch as she is the "common mother" of them all. His appeal comes in the form of a rhetorical question: "Why should we not all together look to her as *our common Mother*, who prays for the unity of God's family and who 'precedes' us all at the head of the long line of witnesses of faith in the one Lord, the Son of God, who was conceived in her virginal womb by the power of the Holy Spirit?" (30).

Evangelicals have been deeply concerned that Rome's Marian dogmas cast a shadow upon the sufficiency of the intercession of Jesus Christ and detract from the worship

1. References are to paragraphs of the encyclical *Redemptoris Mater*.

that Christ alone deserves. They will therefore be convinced that Mary can be the means to advance church unity only if the Marian doctrines rest on a solid support in Scripture. It is therefore necessary to look intently at this recent official statement on Mary with the biblical record in mind.

Mary, says John Paul, is the model for the faithful. She was the first to believe in Jesus, and she was blessed because she believed (12). Her faith preceded even that of the apostolic witness (27). She, the Queen of the Universe, is the model of virtues, the Star of the Sea to guide those who are on the journey of life (6). She was, in the mystery of Christ, present even before the creation of the world (8). In an entirely special and exceptional way she was united to Christ (8). In her the hypostatic vision (of God and man in Jesus Christ) is accomplished and fulfilled (9). She showed the heroic obedience of faith at the cross (18) and her life was hid with Christ in God (17). She was perfectly united with Christ in his self-emptying (18). She became a sharer in the mystery of Christ in every extension of her earthly journey (19). The mother of God is already the eschatological fulfillment of the church (6).

John Paul reaches the apex of his veneration of Mary when he explains the meaning of the ancient icons of the Virgin such as of Our Lady of Vladimir in what is now the Soviet Union: "In these Icons the Virgin shines as the image of divine beauty, the abode of Eternal Wisdom, the figure of one who prays, the prototype of contemplation, the image of glory: she who even in her earthly life possessed the spiritual knowledge inaccessible to human reasoning and who attained through faith the most sublime knowledge" (33). The key to finding all these virtues of faith in Mary is the union in her of grace and faith: the "fulness of grace" that the angel ascribed to her at the annunciation and the faith with which Mary responded, for "blessed is she who believes," set the stage for her entire earthly ministry. In her the "obedience of faith" found perfect realization (13). If as being full of grace "she has been eternally present in the mystery of Christ, through faith she has become a sharer in that mystery in every expression of her earthly journey" (19).

Moreover, what she did in her earthly journey she continues to do in heaven, for she is still present today within mankind (19). Mary's motherhood in the Holy Spirit enables her with maternal love to cooperate in the birth and development of the sons and daughters of Mother Church (44). She was the Mediatrix at the incarnation and will be again at the final coming (41).

This "key" that consists of God's grace and Mary's faith in correlation explains the entirety of Mary's life on earth as well as her continued activity in heaven. It allows the Church of Rome to present her as the Mediatrix (under Christ) both in the procurement as well as the application of redemption. It explains why at every juncture in the Gospels and in the Book of Acts where she is mentioned she is presented in an active role.

In commenting on the incident in the temple, when Jesus at age twelve rebuked Mary and Joseph by saying "Did you not know that I must be in my Father's house?" the encyclical states that even Mary "to whom had been revealed most completely the mystery of his divine sonship, lived in intimacy with this mystery only through faith" (17).

At Cana, Mary, the mother of Jesus, contributed to the beginning of the signs that showed Jesus to be the Messiah (21) and showed her maternal care (22). Later, when the woman in the crowd called out to Jesus: "Blessed is the womb that bore you and the breasts that you sucked,"

(Luke 11:29 RSV) there flashed out in the crowd, at least for a moment, the gospel of the infancy of Christ. Jesus' reply to her, "Blessed rather are those who hear the word of God and obey it" (11:28 RSV), was only to "direct attention from motherhood understood only as a fleshly bond, in order to direct it towards those mysterious bonds of the Spirit which develop from hearing and keeping God's word" (21). Lest anyone think Jesus was warning against a cult of Mary, we are told that Mary was the first of "those who hear the word of God and do it" (21). Venerating Mary was precisely what he desired!

Again, at the cross, when Jesus brought John and Mary together, he highlighted a new relationship between mother and son and between Mary and humanity. It was there that Mary's motherhood of the human race was "clearly stated and established" (23). Finally, in the upper room with the disciples after the resurrection, Mary was at hand in the mystery of the church, in which she continued to be a maternal presence (24). At Pentecost she was present as "an exceptional witness to the mystery of Christ" (27).

Evangelicals understand the gospel to mean that Mary's contribution (sufficient indeed to warrant that we call her blessed) was limited largely to the events surrounding the incarnation. She was the mother of God, and all ages of believers will acknowledge her as such, but after she made this once-for-all-time contribution, she, like John the Baptist, had to decrease as Christ increased. This, rather than the Catholic key of the correlation of fullness of grace and the perfection of faith, will much more adequately explain Mary's role in God's plan of redemption.

Thus at the temple with the boy Jesus, Mary had to withstand a rebuke, and to call her action there an expression of faith is unwarranted. Again in Cana, Jesus had to tell her that he was not ready to act as she had suggested. When the woman in the crowd extolled Mary's blessedness, he not only showed the equality of all true believers but he also indicated that the blessing of all consists in their hearing and doing the will of God. His words serve as a warning to the church not to elevate Mary above the place where God put her. Likewise, Jesus said that his family was not his biotic brothers and sisters who had no more claim to him than anyone else—but those in the crowd who obeyed his voice.

At the cross of Jesus Mary was surely consumed with grief, but she was there only in a passive way. She did not minister to Jesus; rather, he took care of her. In the upper room, whatever she did was not worthy of mention by the Gospel writers. Her role diminishes to the non-mentionable as Christ approached the depths of his re-demptive suffering.

In the apostolic witness, there are only two references to her. Paul spoke of the seed born of a woman (Gal. 4:4), and John told of the woman clothed with the sun who brought forth the manchild (Rev. 12:1). Both depict the birth of Jesus. Nowhere do the apostles allude to her as an exceptional witness to the mystery of Christ. The alleged active role of Mary in the early church must be understood therefore as reading into the text what is simply not there.

If Mary's active role in procuring salvation must be limited to her part as the handmaiden of the Lord, namely, to give birth to the holy child Jesus, then surely her acclaimed mediation in the application of salvation must be seen as also without biblical warrant. For this teaching lacks biblical basis and can only be described as speculation.

Will the encyclical *Redemptoris Mater* advance the unity of the churches? It may advance the unity of the Orthodox churches of the East with the Catholic church of the West, for in all of them Mary is venerated. But it will likely not draw many Protestants closer to Rome. In fact, many will look on Rome's view of Mary as Mariolatry.

Prospects of any convergence in this area of the church's teaching are therefore not bright. The concern of the evangelicals in Singapore is as deep as ever: Marian dogma continues to cast a dark shadow over the saving efficacy of Jesus Christ. These shadows must first be driven away by the light of the Scriptures before evangelicals will feel drawn to embrace the Church of Rome.

Paul G. Schrotenboer
March 1988

Annotated Bibliography

Abbott, Walter M., and Joseph Gallagher. *The Documents of Vatican II*. New York: Guild, 1966. A unique collection of translations into English of council documents, together with selected subsequent Roman documents that amplify, elucidate, or apply the major themes of the Vatican Council constitutions, decrees, and other major pronouncements.

Berkouwer, G. C. *The Second Vatican Council and the New Catholicism*. Grand Rapids: Eerdmans, 1965. A critical analysis of basic theological issues involved in the discussions and decisions of Vatican II from a Reformed perspective.

Denzinger, H., and A. Schönmetzer. *Enchiridion Symbolorum*. Freiburg im Breisgau: Herder, 1965. A complete catalog of official teachings of the Roman Catholic Church from early in the Christian era to modern times.

Eagleson, John, and Philip Scharper, editors. *Puebla and Beyond*. Translated by John Drury. Maryknoll, N.Y.: Orbis, 1979. The text of the Third Conference of Latin American Bishops with background and analysis.

Gaffney, Patrick. *Mary's Spiritual Maternity According to St. Louis de Montfort*. Bay Shore, N.Y.: Montfort, 1976. This work attempts to delve into the foundations of the spiritual maternity as taught by Saint Louis de Montfort and into his Mariology.

Luther, Martin. "Vorlesungen über Mose" *(D. Martin Luthers Werken*, Teil 42–44). Weimar: Hermann Böhlaus

Nachfolger, 1911–15. Luther's lectures on the first five books of the Old Testament.

Padilla, C. René, editor. *The New Face of Evangelicalism: An International Symposium on the Lausanne Covenant.* Downers Grove: Inter-Varsity, 1976.

Schillebeeckx, Edward. *Kerkelijk ambt.* Bloemendaal: Nelissen, 1980. A discussion of ecclesiastical offices within the Roman Catholic tradition from the viewpoint of the "new theology" within Roman Catholicism.

U.S. Lutheran-Roman Catholic Dialogue. Justification by Faith, in *Origins*, NC Documentary Service, October 6, 1983, vol. 13, no. 17.

Index